INTERNET MARKETING
FOR THE REST OF US

YOUR IN-DEPTH GUIDE TO
PROFITABLE POPULARITY

RACHNA JAIN, PsyD

FOREWORD BY ANDREA J. LEE
INTRODUCTION BY DAVE LAKHANI

Internet Marketing for the Rest of Us: Your Guide to Profitable Popularity

Copyright © 2013 Rachna Jain, PysD

All rights reserved. No portion of this book may be reproduced mechanically, electronically, or by any other means, including photocopying, without written permission of the publisher. It is illegal to copy this book, post it to a website, or distribute it by any other means without permission from the publisher.

ISBN-10: 1-60087-004-X
ISBN-13: 978-1-60087-004-0

Rachna Jain, PsyD
20203 Goshen Road #374
Gaithersburg, MD 20879
http://ProfitablePopularity.com

Limits of Liability and Disclaimer of Warranty
The author and publisher shall not be liable for your misuse of this material. This book is strictly for informational and educational purposes.

Warning – Disclaimer
The purpose of this book is to educate and entertain. The author and/or publisher do not guarantee that anyone following these techniques, suggestions, tips, ideas, or strategies will become successful. The author and/or publisher shall have neither liability nor responsibility to anyone with respect to any loss or damage caused, or alleged to be caused, directly or indirectly by the information contained in this book.

Cover Art: Erin Ferree, BrandStyleDesign.com
Interior Design: Delaine Ulmer, StudioUltimateDesign.com

PRAISE FOR
Internet Marketing For the Rest Of Us

"In Internet Marketing for the Rest of Us: Your In-Depth Guide to Profitable Popularity, Dr. Jain cuts through all the internet marketing noise with one simple question. For a business owner, it's the only question: How much money is internet marketing making for you?

If you've been making yourself crazy with your internet marketing, trying to keep up with the constant changes and still trying to run your business, then this book is for you. Get out a highlighter and a pad of sticky notes. Dr. Jain shows you how to use the Internet to obtain the measurable results that are appropriate for your business model.

Easy to follow and implement, this book will be instrumental in planning out your internet marketing goals, establishing benchmarks and setting your business firmly on the path to profitable popularity."

~*Barbara Grassey*
www.TheMarketingWord.com

"Rachna, you have amazing insight into what's needed in this fast-changing digital environment. I'm grateful for all your wisdom, mad skills, and big heart!"

~*Mark Silver*
www.HeartofBusiness.com

"Want to use Internet Marketing to do REAL good in the world without playing all the Internet Marketing Games to do it?

Me too. And now, thanks to Rachna Jain, we can.

What you hold in your hand are the key's to a rarified (and often abused) kingdom - a treasure trove of fresh thinking and straight talk that transforms mind-numbing mechanics into easy-to-use super-tools, and boring business basics into a stunningly simple path to unleashed impact and sustainable profitability.

And who in the world doesn't want more of that?"

~Lissa Boles
www.TheSoulMap.com

"As a busy and in demand speaker, the question I have always asked myself is "How can I serve more people without being constantly on the road?" I knew the short answer was 'online" but what does that mean? I had NO idea of where to get started, and honestly the words "online marketing" felt a little bit like watching a late night infomercial.

Enter my Fairy On-line God mother, aka Rachna. She asked questions, wanted to know about my business, what my goals were and put together an action plan customized to meet my needs.

Now I have a plan that makes sense, and people that were always looking for me, actually find me! It had had a huge IMPACT on my business and yes, dare I say, profitability.

If you truly want to help people looking for your services actually find you, you absolutely need to read, and apply the lessons from this book."

~Shawn Shepheard
www.SugarFreeShawn.com

"Finally!!! A no-hype book that tells the truth about how to be successful at Internet Marketing!

This book is for you if you have a love-hate relationship with online marketing. If you want more clients and income...and, at the same time, feel that online marketing is a bit slimy, then read this book NOW.

Rachna Jain takes a technically and emotionally complex subject and, with humor and love, helps us to know exactly what to do (and not do) next.

Read this for instant clarity and relief.

I predict this is the new Internet Bible for "the rest of us." It will soothe you when times are tough...help you find relief when you are doing (or worrying) too much - and oh yes, help you to be more profitable and popular. This book is my new fave!"

~**Casey Truffo**
www.BeAWealthyTherapist.com

"Rachna makes the technical stuff easy to understand and implement."

~**Jennifer Lee**
www.RightBrainBusinessPlan.com

"This book will save so many businesses! If this book had been around when I'd started my business, it would have saved me years and hundreds of thousands of dollars of building my business backwards. Rachna's book showed me exactly where I went astray and where to concentrate to make the biggest difference - and eliminated a lot of my internet overwhelm!"

~**Erin Ferree**
www.BrandStyleDesign.com

Dear Ciel,
May you always be profitable AND popular! :) Rachna

ACKNOWLEDGMENTS

I ALWAYS FIND it a bit overwhelming to write acknowledgments like this, mostly, I think, from the fear of forgetting to mention someone who is so important to me, and that omission being evident for everyone to see.

However, taking a deep breath, I'm going to attempt it. I've made the list and checked it twice. If I somehow still missed someone, I'm so sorry and know that I am thankful and appreciative for you, too.

This is a bit of a longer list, because I'm blessed by knowing so many great people!

To my mother, Usha, for teaching me how to be independent, to think for myself, and to be a high achiever. Thanks Mom!

To my father, Daya, for teaching me the value of hard work and persistence.

To my husband, Mike, for sharing your life with me and for all the times we laugh. I appreciate how you show up for me, and us, each and every day.

To my brother Deepak, for all the history we share, and the love and care you bring to all that you do. I'm happy that I'll soon be gaining Margot as a sister-in-law.

To Andrea J. Lee, for being my friend, colleague, thought partner, and mentor. I learn so much from spending time with you and developing new ideas with you. I love how you think and I'm so glad you're in my life. I also really love your Mr. Big joke.

To Dave Lakhani, for being my friend, thought partner, and life catalyst. I value so much your deep acceptance of me and the unconstrained freedom you give me to think my thoughts out loud. I've learned so much through our connection.

To Jodi Cummins, for being my friend since graduate school and my partner in crime. I'm so thankful for your lasting friendship and all the fun stuff we've done. I especially love how you make up your own song lyrics.

To Selvy Thiruvengadam, for being my friend since I was twelve, and for growing up with me. We're the kind of friends who easily pick up again, right where we left off. Thank you for that.

To Forrest Wright, for our many years of friendship. Thank you for your super cutting edge style when we went to my Junior Prom. Can't wait to drink your homemade margaritas!

To Denise Wakeman for your friendship and support.

To Susan Conrad Guiher, for being my first coaching buddy and all the great conversations we shared when we were conspiring to share coaching with the world.

To French, Ona, and Lynn for being part of my personal health and life balance team. Thank you for helping me stay healthy, happy, and mostly sane.

To Casey Truffo, Lissa Boles, Lisa Murrell, and Mark Silver, for being willing to take the first step in working with me. Your initial confidence and trust in me has helped accelerate my success.

ACKNOWLEDGMENTS

Thank you, too, to all my other clients - you let me do work I love, each and every day.

To Mary Jane Stern, for being on my team for so many years, and being such an asset to my business.

To Chelsea and Team Solamar, for helping me turn my creative ideas into reality.

To Jen Gibson and Kristi Shymr, for helping to keep things going, whatever it takes.

To my previous coaches: Lynne Hornyak, Terri Levine, and Michael Port. Thank you for sharing your wisdom with me in my journey to find my own.

To Barbara Grassey for her fast and thorough editing.

To Erin Ferree for the beautiful cover design and internal illustrations.

To Delaine Ulmer for her confident and gorgeous layout.

To Linda Richey for her wonderful fable illustrations.

To the ladies who drink (AKA book club), for our monthly meetings with book discussion and wine. Lots of wine.

To all the awesome people in the Wealthy Thought Leader family - too many to name here, but I appreciate all of you. Thank you for being part of my circle.

Thank you to all my Facebook friends who make me laugh each day. You make working solo much more fun!

And to you, dear reader. My goal for this book is to show you what's possible, and what you might do differently, without making you feel inadequate. I hope to inspire you to make whatever changes you must to have the life and business you want. Let me know how I did!

xoxo,

Rachna

CONTENTS

Acknowledgements .... *vii*
Foreword .... *xiii*
Introduction .... *xvii*

Internet Marketing is Broken 23
The Tree & The Sorceress Fable 37
Popularity vs. Profitability vs. Both 53
What You Need For a Marketing Plan 65
Cash Flow Makes Your Business Go 77
Critical Thinking in Your Business 91
Business Clarity 103
Business Resilience is Vital 113
Becoming a Category of One 121
The Seven Social Currencies of Online Marketing 133
Metrics & Measurement in Your Business 151
The Profitable Popularity Method 169
Creating and Using Content 173
Generating Traffic 193
Building Your Authority Website 209
Your Content Money Spirals 219
Case Studies 233
Your Business As a Force For Good 245
Putting It All Together 253

Book Resource Center *257*
About the Author *259*

FOREWORD

I REMEMBER WHEN the magnitude of what the Internet would mean really landed. With a gasp, my brain latched onto what this tool would mean for us. By us, I mean smart business owners with great ideas to serve the world and the will to DO something about them.

There were actually two moments. The first was when I earned my first commission check for a piece of work I'd obtained and delivered 100% through my website in 1998. And the second was when I and the 3 and a half person team at CoachVille, an online coach training business, celebrated breaking the $3 million dollar revenue mark in 2003.

This was really big! If so few people could serve nearly 40,000 people in such a short amount of time, what could the population of the planet do? This was a win for the good guys and nothing was going to stop us now.

Much has evolved since then. The territory of the Internet has been explored, gambled on, used for good and bad (and everything in between) and certainly plumbed to its depth for potential. Some would say it's changed everything, and they would be right.

The problem though, is that for every hour of positive action that gets taken by someone with Internet access, dozens of hours are wasted through confusion, ignorance, misinformation, outright manipulation and even the well-intentioned creation of plain old "info-crap." As a business coach with, at last count, over 10,000 hours of coaching under her belt, I know first hand how much agony the promise of success via the Internet can bring – particularly when it remains stubbornly out of reach.

At worst, it can be like the promise of sunshine on the other side of prison bars, and many years can be wasted trying to make sense of it. How many dollars do we think have been invested, how many countless hours of energy spent, only to end up with websites that do nothing?

The saying goes, "Hope is not a strategy to build a business on" but that hasn't stopping anyone from trying.

Enter Internet Marketing for the Rest of Us: Your In-Depth Guide to Profitable Popularity written by Dr. Rachna Jain, a dear friend, thought partner and someone I've had the privilege of seeing create concrete results for an eye-poppingly wide range of business owners using what she shares in this book. I believe what she's put on these pages is the cure for what has ailed the Internet for small business owners, or as close to it as you'll find between two covers.

In reading it, you'll find information and context presented in a way that's sensible, digestible, concrete and rewarding to take action on. Flashes of insight populate each chapter like friendly "ahas" slapping you on the back. At once a thinking book and a tactical one, I'm very grateful to now be able to recommend it to people. Frankly, it's an overdue book that I sense will bring with it a lot of healing.

FORWARD

Personally, in reviewing the book, I was led to logical conclusions that enabled me to simplify business strategy, whittle down wasteful processes, and make clearer, quicker decisions about things that haven't been working. It's already saved and earned my businesses a noteworthy amount of time, money and energy, and I know it will continue to do so because I intend to come back to the book again and again.

As you dig in, prepare to reap the harvest of the right actions, and the right thinking at just the right time – just be prepared to do more than read. Whether you intend to or not, with Rachna's words and experience as your guides, you'll also become a much smarter online business owner, both profitable AND popular, at last!

Andrea J. Lee
Author, Multiple Streams of Coaching Income
CEO, Wealthy Thought Leader

INTRODUCTION

BEFORE I WROTE this, I browsed Facebook, checked my Twitter Feed and looked at a couple of messages on LinkedIn. I saw pictures of people's breakfasts, videos of absurd cats and cute babies and in between it all I found out about a new piece of technology from a post by a blogger I like that will transform my workday. I got all that from people I "know." Some of those people I really do know and some are just people I have a relationship with online. Many of those people are looking through all the messages they get for a message from me too because they know me, like me, trust me. They hope that I'll bring them something useful today, something they can hang onto, something that will allow them to know me just a little better.

Let's face it, if you are like most average business owners you really don't get the point of why people post pictures of sunsets and breakfast on Facebook. The pictures are pretty but are they profitable? You ask yourself, "Do I really care, and couldn't that person have done something more productive with their time?"

It often appears that social media has devolved into a popularity contest with people vying for likes and follows instead of actual connection and engagement. Often the most liked and followed are the most self absorbed and narcissistic. And all that leaves us wondering, "What's the point?"

But popularity does have a purpose and it turns out done properly, a profitable one.

Dr. Jain digs deep into the ethos of social media for answers to how to create profitable popularity. It turns out profitable popularity is not inane or unachievable. And, as it turns out, big numbers of followers aren't always desirable. It is the most connected followers and friends and likes that create profitability in social media.

I've had the good fortune of knowing Rachna for many years now. I've watched her and occasionally participated as she's explored the social media landscape from its early beginning through the lens of a psychologist, a marketer, a business owner, and as a participant. I've appreciated her scientific approach to understanding why people do what they do online and her thorough study of the applications of social media inside business. Rachna is able to move easily through a mix of messaging and media that spans intellectual, psychological, business and personal that works seamlessly every day. And, in this book, she shows you how to do the very same thing in a voice that really is her own. As I read, it was like having a compelling conversation that moves easily from technical to personal to insightful, then funny. It makes the experience complete and memorable.

As you read the chapters of this book, you'll cut through the hoopla and discover the exact formula for turning a popularity contest into something connected and measurable.

The biggest mistake business owners and those hoping to find profit in social media make is forgetting that social media is a distribution channel, not a cure all to end all.

INTRODUCTION

If you are old enough to remember the time of television before cable TV, you'll remember that there were only a few channels and each channel had different programming. Sometimes the programming was designed to compete head on with the programming on another channel and was different and sometimes it competed by being very similar. The goal though was to get you to stay on that channel and not go to the competing channel. Today, because of the multitude of channels that cover the same topic (I'm pretty sure there are 300 ESPN channels now) in order to get to profitability programmers rely on popularity of their hosts or over the top programming storylines that cause people to talk at the water cooler or the virtual water cooler of social media. They do it not because they are trying to push the boundaries of good taste or art. They do it to get attention to the very thing that makes them profitable, the advertisement.

Social media is simply a mass distribution platform that allows virtually anyone to create programming that gathers attention. If your story is compelling enough to maintain the attention of those people who find you interesting they stay. Done well, they not only stay and watch but they interact and become bit actors in your unfolding story. And as they interact with you, their friends and neighbors and connections watch and sometimes interact as well. They directly comment, post, ask questions, engage.

And that is the one thing that television, newspaper or radio could never do and it is where your opportunity lies.

By creating a compelling and engaging story inside the distribution channel of social media you capture the imagination and attention of people who like you or who like your products and services. If you can educate them, connect with them or be their intellectual entertainment, you own their attention for a brief moment. If in that brief moment you can move them emotionally, you can move them profitably.

Most companies don't know how to do that today but as you dig into this book you'll begin to understand the process.

It turns out there are seven currencies of social media that you must understand if you hope to successfully leverage social media. There are also fourteen specific strategies that will transform how you market online today.

And as you'll discover, profitable popularity isn't just about people loving you; it is also about the search engines loving you, too. As social media becomes search and search becomes social, you must adapt to reach the audiences who want to connect with you but don't know you exist yet.

The path is very direct: Content, Traffic, Monetization. But real success is found in the nuances and this book contains what all the other books on social media left out.

Dr. Jain brings together something in this book that has been missing from all the discussion of social media so far and that is the psychology of social media. She speaks from the experience of a psychologist and social scientist. She demonstrates for you how to control the delicate interaction that occurs between seller and buyer, business and prospect.

If you build it, they won't necessarily come; but if you lead through engagement they will follow. That's the marketing that works today. It's where you find your true fans, your loyal customers and it's where you create a connection through your customers to prospects you could never reach before, their friends who are just like them. You can reach them now because they've given you access to a platform where they congregate; they only ask that you provide them with something interesting, useful, and relevant before you show them something they can buy. And if you do, they will buy. But beware! If you act like a pushy car salesman from television they will react in force because the distribution channel carries messages in two directions, from you to them and from them to everyone else.

In the old days of television, radio, and newspaper as distribution channels, it was hard for a disgruntled customer to buy an ad to take on the big company that abused them. Today

INTRODUCTION

it just takes a few strokes of keys on a computer and the world as we know it changes.

Never has access to the minds and emotions of so many been so accessible.

You are only pages away from creating a strategy that will transform the way you do business and the way you engage clients and prospects. Rachna makes the path to profitable popularity clear and easy to follow.

Who will you connect with profitably today?

Dave Lakhani
Author, Persuasion: The Art of Getting What You Want

Chapter 1

INTERNET MARKETING IS BROKEN

INTERNET MARKETING IS broken.

And it needs to be fixed.

As someone who has worked online since 1997, which is practically the start of the modern Internet, I've witnessed many changes in the online marketing space.

Early on, the Internet was a cash machine. Since competition was so minimal, early Internet marketers were putting up quick sites and making sales. The barrier to entry on the Internet was higher at that time. You needed to have a decent computer and something faster than a dial-up Internet connection. You needed to know how to set up a web page, likely using HTML, and you needed to set up a system to take payments on your website. You had to set up mechanisms for delivering your product, and you needed to have a way to retain and re-engage with clients.

All of those steps are still needed today, but the difference now is that it is much easier to do. Now, there are many premade template and website building services. You can more easily hire people to build your website for you, or with a few hours of time, you can put out a reasonable template by yourself. When I first began working online, the technology didn't exist to easily put audio on your website—and never mind video. Now, though, you can easily create a video from your smartphone and upload it to the Internet with little time gap and not a lot of expense. Similarly, you have many ways to take payments now and many options for delivering your product or service. Conference bridge-lines used to be prohibitively expensive where now you can get them for free. In a way of describing it, there has been a democratization of resources. Now, everyone from the young teen to the savvy senior can find a way to get online and sell their ideas or products. Current estimates suggest that there are more than 181 million blogs online today, and that this number doubles every six months. Easy access to resources is enabling more people, young and old, to venture online.

Perhaps this graphic will help illustrate:

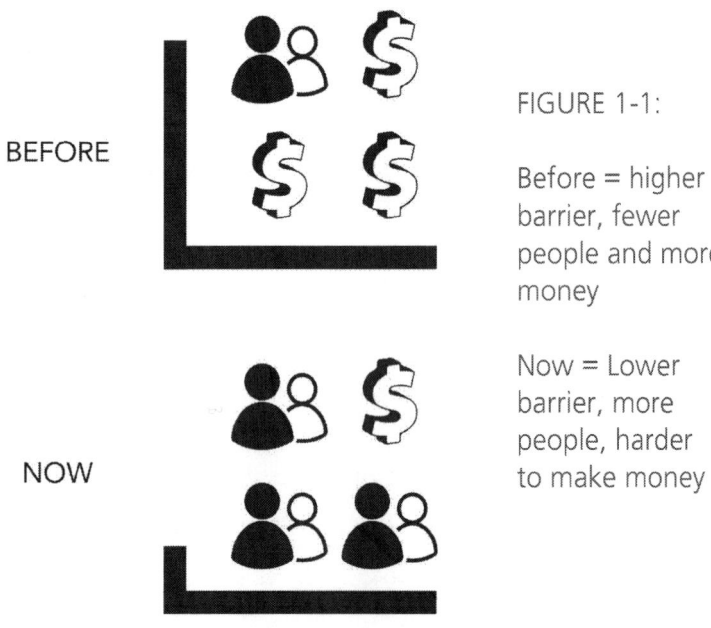

FIGURE 1-1:

Before = higher barrier, fewer people and more money

Now = Lower barrier, more people, harder to make money

The online marketspace is getting more and more crowded, and it is becoming more difficult to stand out.

A few years ago, Jupiter Research reported that more than 50% of online consumers consult a blog before making an online purchasing decision. So, as a business owner, you clearly need to be online, and you must be able to get attention.

Attention has always been the currency of the online marketspace. The trouble is online attention has become in short supply, not to mention jaded and mistrustful.

Many socially-conscious business owners are struggling to be heard.

The typical Internet user is becoming savvier. They are more skilled at using the Internet to gather data and to research and drive forward their life and purchasing decisions.

This increased Internet use has led to a rise in "social decision making," which refers to the way that people decide to make purchases.

The first thing to understand about social decision making is that we all want to make the best choices we can, using the least effort possible.

How we purchase goods and services has changed as the Internet has become more accessible.

For example, in the past, if you were considering the purchase of a new set of luggage, your purchasing process likely went something like this: first, you'd visit the store and see and test the luggage for yourself. You might ask the salesperson for his or her recommendation. You might come home and call your close friends or family to ask them what kind of luggage they liked best. Ultimately, you would make the best decision you could based on the information you gained.

Now, although you still may do each of those steps, you are also very likely to go online to read reviews and recommendations, and perhaps, also, to shop for a lower price while you're there.

In reading reviews and recommendations, you are utilizing the wisdom of the crowd—after all, if 2,436 people liked this luggage and gave it 4.5 stars, chances are high you'll like it too. In this scenario, you are using the opinions of people you don't know and never met to help you make a better purchasing decision.

This process is a way of reducing our personal stress and cognitive load about making buying decisions and using the knowledge of the crowd to help us make the best decision with the least amount of effort.

Social decision making is a process which is influenced by social proof. This is one reason that case studies, testimonials, and other ways that you can demonstrate rather than tell about the value of your services are vital.

In the past, bold hype and exaggerated claims, complete with flashy pictures of beach homes and fancy cars were the way products were sold online. Now, as the online marketing space opens up to all different types of people, there is less and less response to the dramatic, in-your-face, used-car-salesman type of Internet marketing tactics. While these still work in some markets, they don't seem to work as well as they used to, and in some markets, they never have—and won't—work at all. This creates an opening—a possibility—in the way that you might market online. You need not feel that you have to use dramatic and over-the-top marketing in order to be heard.

At the same time, simply having a nice looking website and providing good service or products isn't enough. This is not a "build it and they will come" type of scenario. You can't just put up a website and provide good service and expect that clients will find you and hire you.

You must know how to master the technologies of marketing online and be able to adapt to this ever-changing frontier.

CHAPTER 1

> **SPECIFICALLY, YOU MUST KNOW**
> How to gain attention—visibility;
> How to generate engagement—credibility;
> How to build community and create influence;
> And how to sell your services and products.

Even though heart-centered business owners rarely resort to the same kinds of tactics that old-style Internet marketers use, I still think that Internet marketing is broken for heart-centered marketers, too.

I believe this because there are so many soulful business owners who put up websites but don't know how to use them effectively to build visibility, engagement, influence, and to make money. To put it directly: There are business owners who spend thousands of dollars they don't have to building an online presence nobody ever visits.

They worry more about the shape of the letters in their logo than they think about how they will use their online presence to build their businesses. They spend more time considering hundreds of ideas than they do in acting on even one.

This is a problem.

When did it become OK to invest so much in infrastructure that you don't even use properly? Why invest so much in a website that does nothing more for you than function as a pretty brochure? What is your website for if it's not helping your business grow and prosper?

And where did you get the idea that putting up a website was simply a "If I build it, they will come" kind of deal?

Would you ever spend thousands of dollars on something for your home if you had no idea how to use it? Would you ever spend thousands of dollars to buy something if you didn't know what you were getting?

If the answer is no (and I really hope it's no), then how does it makes sense to spend so much on an online presence if you don't know how to use it or what it can do for you?

That just doesn't make sense.

There are business owners who spend thousands of dollars they don't have to building an online presence nobody ever visits.

Why is it that socially-conscious business owners who want to do good in the world and make a big impact on improving the world shy away from Internet marketing like it was some kind of pestilence or plague?

That doesn't make sense either.

In a talk I gave last year, I asked the heart-centered audience what they thought about traffic—traffic being a way of describing the flow of visitors to your website. In that room of about 150 people, with an additional 300 or so viewing online, I asked the audience what they thought about traffic. I asked how many of them felt that Internet marketing was icky? More than 70% of the people raised their hands. I asked how many of them felt they were here to make a bigger impact than they currently were. Again, about 70% percent of them raised their hands. (And some even raised both hands on both questions, not sure how to accurately count that.)

I then said this: "If you think traffic is icky, and you're not making the impact you want, these two beliefs are related. Without Internet traffic, you'll never have the biggest impact you can have. And you'll never make as much money as you can make."

Most simply, the reason for this is that if you're not reaching enough people, you can't make as much difference.

We'll get into more detail about this later in the book, in the section where we talk about the three kinds of traffic, but for now, the main takeaway is that without Internet traffic, your website isn't producing for you like it could.

One of the biggest hurdles to online marketing for soulopreneurs is their own belief system about Internet marketing being icky, yucky, and "forcing" people to do something.

Yet the truth is Internet marketing is a set of tools which by themselves are neither good nor bad.

For example, if you look around your house right now, you'll see a lot of tools. In your kitchen, you'll see knives for cutting food and forks for eating food. In your bathroom, you'll see toothbrushes for cleaning your teeth, and in your garage you'll see a snow blower, pressure washer, and chainsaw. (At least in my garage, anyway. My husband uses them.)

If you think about it, a knife can be helpful when it's cutting a piece of fruit. It can be hurtful when it slips and cuts your finger. A fork can be helpful when it's letting you enjoy your favorite food. It can be hurtful when your child is threatening to poke him or herself in the eye with it.

Do you see where I'm going with this? Tools are neutral—they can be good or bad depending on how they are used.

When you look around your house, you don't immediately call knives and forks bad or pressure washers good. Their value to you depends on their purpose.

Internet marketing tools are just like the knives and forks and toothbrushes and snow blowers. They help us accomplish what we want to do more easily, faster and better.

There are many ways to market your business online and to do it in an ethical and comfortable way. The biggest mistake you can make is ignoring the Internet as a viable marketing channel for your business just because it feels mysterious or makes you uncomfortable. Your website can—and should—function as more than a pretty brochure.

But you need to be open to learning how the Internet works. You need to be willing to learn what you don't know (and no, you don't have to learn everything all at once). You need to be willing to be a little bit uncomfortable and stretch yourself in order to have the kind of business and the kind of impact you are called to create.

Otherwise, you're just wasting money on your pretty website, social media icons, and pretty graphics.

The second biggest mistake heart-centered business owners make is thinking that if they began marketing online, they would be inundated and overwhelmed by so many offers and so many requests that they couldn't accommodate them all.

With more than 90% of the clients I've worked with, this doesn't actually occur. Remember how I said that the online marketspace was getting more and more crowded, and we each have to work harder to get attention? Online marketing generally takes some time to show results. I'm not advocating, as much, the sudden big launch approach, where you throw yourself into creating massive buzz and presence almost instantaneously. First, that is exhausting to do over and over, and is not, ultimately, sustainable. Second, with the time-shifted nature of social media and the time it takes to gain search engine positioning, it is likely that your online marketing will take a little bit of time to show results.

You're more likely to feel concerned it's not working than you are to be overwhelmed with a sudden influx of more business than you can handle.

It's important to understand that a certain amount of online marketing focuses on educating your potential client, and this education process usually takes some time.

So once you understand that technology is just a set of tools, and that you're not likely to be overwhelmed with business just as you begin marketing online, the third piece to understand is how the Internet is reshaping our networks and connections.

We already touched on this a bit around social decision making, and there are other ways that the Internet is reshaping how we relate.

I believe that the Internet is reshaping our attention, memory, and ways of connecting.

One interesting phenomenon is microfragmentation.

In my way of using this word, it means that the size and searchability of the Internet is making it possible for people to self-select into smaller and smaller groups.

When the Internet first began, there were many fewer people using it. And it could be difficult to find other people like you, unless you were part of the gaming, programming, or other usually male, highly-technical group who began congregating online using bulletin boards and user groups.

Now, as the Internet has become larger and more diverse, and as searchability on the Internet has also improved, you can more and more easily find others who share in your diverse interests, no matter how rare or random they might be.

You can find more and more of your people with greater and greater degrees of specificity.

I raise this here because there are many business owners who have no idea of the depth and specificity with which they can make connections online. They mistakenly believe that "their people"—meaning their target audience or target customers—are not looking online to find them.

I completely disagree. Certainly, your target audience might not be using the same exact words to find you as you would use yourself, but I assure you they are looking. They might not know of your specialized vocabulary to describe what you do, but they are definitely looking for you.

It's a mistake to think that your business offerings are so mysterious and unknowable that they are not being searched for online. Of course, people may not be searching for exactly what you do in exactly the way you do it, but they are very likely searching for the results your services provide.

Let me see if I can explain this with an example.

Let's take a fictional business owner, Suzy. Suzy has created a very special energetic healing process which she landed on intuitively, based on inner wisdom and spiritual guidance. Suzy has had great success using this energetic healing on people who have been depressed for many years, and for whom traditional approaches of psychotherapy and medication haven't worked.

Suzy calls her energetic healing process "The Fantastically Amazing Energetic Healing of Two Worlds Brought Together For This Time and Space To Serve The World." (The acronym is TFAEHOTWBTFTTASTSTW.)

Suzy wants to help more people with her energetic healing approach. She comes to me, and our conversation goes something like this:

> SUZY: I really want to reach more people with my work. I know it can help them. But I don't think Internet marketing will work for me.
>
> ME: Why?
>
> SUZY: Because. I invented this technique, and nobody is doing it aside from me.
>
> ME: Right. So, do you think that if more people knew of your technique, you could help them?
>
> SUZY: Yes. But I don't think you can help me because anybody searching for "The Fantastically Amazing Energetic Healing of Two Worlds Brought Together For This Time and Space To Serve The World" has already heard of me because I'm the only one doing this work.

ME: Right. But is it possible that there are people searching for energy healing or healing from depression who would benefit from the TFAEHOTWBTFTTASTSTW, but can't because they haven't heard of you yet and can't find you online?

SUZY: Oh. I see.

Do you see where I'm going with this? It requires a bit of mindset adjustment. You can't know, for sure, if there are people searching for your TFAEHOTWBTFTTASTSTW, but you can make an educated guess that if you've helped some people solve a problem or challenge, there are other people with the same problem or challenge who are seeking a similar solution.

And at least SOME of those people are likely to be interested in your TFAEHOTWBTFTTASTSTW. As a business owner, your goal should be to use Internet marketing strategies to get found whenever a possible client is searching for something you can help them with. You can do this through a combination of search, content, and social media strategies.

You can shape the world of Internet marketing to suit your preferred style of working.

All together, Internet marketing is one of the most stable and most beneficial means for connecting with people looking for solutions to their problems. Later on in this book, I'll give you examples of several real-life, conscious businesses that are using Internet marketing successfully, as well as a step-by-step dissection of one of my six-figure-plus coaching businesses built entirely from Internet marketing.

But before we go any further, I want to make sure that you've understood that your people are looking for you online. They don't know who you are, they don't know what you can do for them specifically, but again, if you've ever helped another person solve a problem or overcome a challenge, there are other people like him or her who would like to have the same results.

If you are not using Internet marketing as one of your business strategies, you will never have the largest and most meaningful impact that you could have.

The three basic meta-skills of any business are to acquire clients, serve clients and retain clients.

When each of these pieces is functioning well, the business is growing steadily, making an impact, and is profitable. It costs about 60% less to retain an existing customer than it costs to generate a new one, so mastering these three skills will make a huge positive difference in your business.

Internet marketing can help you with all three skills.

Learning how to generate visibility and clients from the Internet can be one of the most important business investments you will ever make. When your client acquisition (marketing and sales) system is working properly, your business runs better, is more profitable, and is much more fun. Instead of worrying about where your next client will come from (or if they will ever come at all), you can focus on providing the best service and experience you can offer, turning your clients into raving fans.

You can use the technologies of Internet marketing to better serve your clients, offering additions such as online forums, private Facebook groups, and private membership sites.

You can use the technologies of Internet marketing to retain clients, such as through providing online support, or customer service via social media, or by showcasing your client's success in case study form—which creates a ripple effect of benefit into your business.

When an easily accessible technology can enable you to perform all the functions of your business better and more easily, isn't it worth getting over your discomfort and learning what you need to know to benefit?

As we move ahead, I hope to share with you some new perspectives and approaches to bringing your business online and doing it in a way that feels good and works well for you. You can shape the world of Internet marketing to suit your preferred style of working. But before you can shape it, you must first see its potential and understand fully what it can do for you.

You can't customize what you don't understand.

As we complete this chapter, I want to make sure that you're taking away a few key points.

#1 No matter how different your business is Internet marketing can help all aspects of your business run better and be more profitable.

#2 People are searching online for what you offer.

#3 Being afraid or uncomfortable is not a good reason to avoid Internet marketing.

#4 You will never have the biggest impact you can have without using the Internet.

#5 You can be successful on the Internet by focusing on quality offerings, meaningful content, and personal connection.

Internet marketing is a treasure chest of possibility and opportunity for your business. There are vast riches—monetary, personal, relational—available for you if you will put aside your discomfort and take the first step.

Are you ready?

NOTES

Chapter 2
THE TREE & THE SORCERESS FABLE

SOME OF YOU will understand intuitively this idea of opening your business up to people who are seeking you. For others, it might require another way to look at this idea. Here is a short fable that, I hope, will give you another way to see what I'm describing:

The Tree and the Sorceress: A Fable →

Once upon a time, there was a lovely tree that grew in a beautiful meadow. The tree loved the meadow, and it flourished there.

CHAPTER 2

The tree grew sweet berries which fed the birds. The birds sang happily and filled the meadow with song. The meadow was an alive and beautiful place for a time.

You see, at the edge of this meadow was a dark and forbidden forest in which lived an evil wizard. He was jealous of the beauty of the meadow and of the beautiful tree that lived there. He cast an evil spell on the meadow like evil wizards do. The meadow began to die.

CHAPTER 2

First, the streams in the meadow began to dry up. Then it stopped raining in the meadow. The tree sucked on its roots harder and deeper trying to find a source of nourishment and supply, but it was no use. Its sweet berries dried up, and the birds stopped singing.

The once beautiful and alive meadow grew silent and dark.

CHAPTER 2

One day, a young sorceress happened to be passing by the meadow. She saw the dark meadow and the once beautiful tree and was saddened. She saw that the evil spell the wizard had cast was like a locked gate around the meadow. Nothing could flow to the tree as long as that locked gate was there.

The sorceress began to think, "What if I could find a way to release the tree from this horrible spell?"

CHAPTER 2

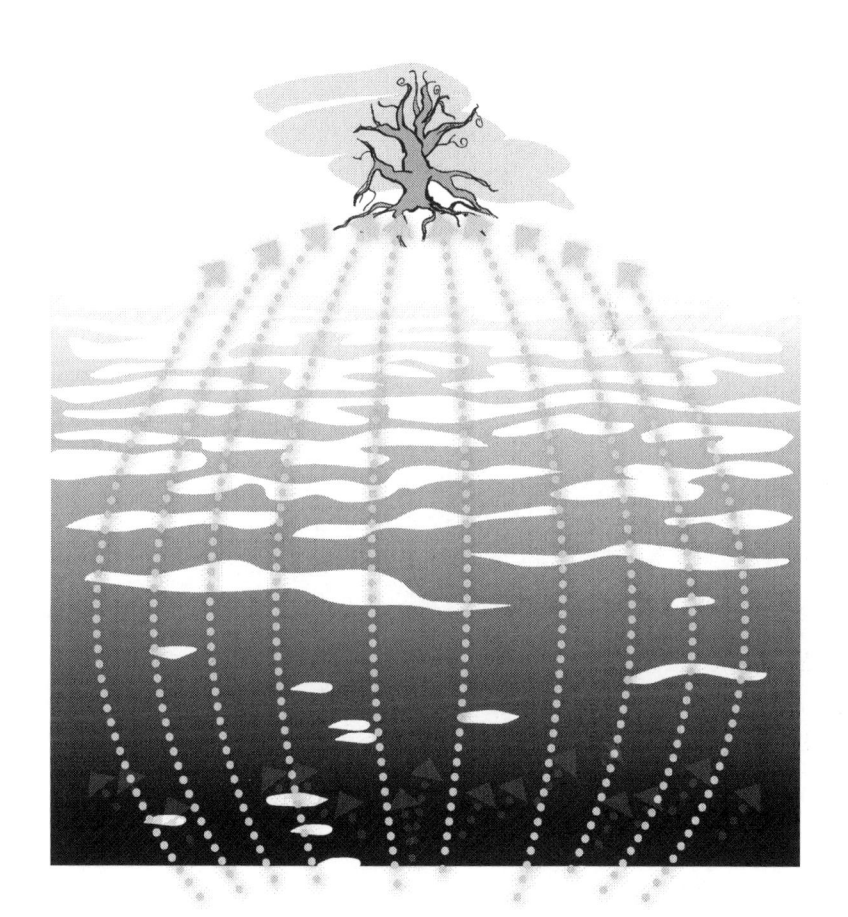

You see, the sorceress knew there was a river just a few hundred feet outside of the meadow. She knew that if she could get help creating multiple streams from the river to the tree, she could break the evil spell.

45

She called on her friend, the King of the Spiders and asked him for help. The King of the Spiders said, "Dear Sorceress, I will call all my subjects together. We will dig channels from the river to the tree. We know of your power and will be glad to assist you in this noblest of tasks."

CHAPTER 2

The King of the Spiders called together all of his subjects and told them of the task, and the spiders began digging.

The sorceress went back to the meadow and cast her best, most powerful, unlocking spell. Although the evil wizard was strong, the sorceress was stronger. With a mighty rumble and a huge crash the evil spell was broken.

At that exact same moment, the spiders completed their work. The pathway to the meadow was open once more, and water gushed into the meadow restoring life to the tree.

With this fresh and ongoing supply of water the tree grew stronger and taller than ever before. Its roots spread deeper. Its branches filled with juicy berries. The birds returned and filled the meadow with song. The tree and the meadow were both alive and beautiful once more.

If you are not using the Internet to help you grow your business, you are operating with a dark spell overcasting your meadow. Your business can't connect with those it is meant to serve.

When I present this fable, I often end with a quote from Arthur C. Clarke: "Any sufficiently advanced technology is indistinguishable from magic."

And, it is true. While using Internet marketing strategies may seem strange and mysterious, once you know how to use them they can create results for you that seem like magic.

NOTES

Chapter 3

POPULARITY VS. PROFITABILITY VS. BOTH

ONE OF THE elements of online marketing that really, really grits my nerves is the over-focus on popularity at the expense of profitability. Let me explain.

In the absence of knowing any other way to proceed, many online business owners focus on building large social networks and measure their success in terms of "friends" or "fans" or "followers." Now, remember how I said that the new measure of Internet marketing success is quality, meaning, and personal connection?

While there are still benefits to creating a large online community, it's not just about popularity anymore. There needs to be a focus on building relationships and creating engagement and dialogue—and a strategic focus on activating your online connections into deeper relationships with you. Stated another way, there has to be a plan for how you will engage strategically in order to generate the best outcomes for the use of your time and resources.

Let me give you an example. With the rise of social media, there is some sense that spending hours and hours a day on the social networks—cultivating hundreds or thousands of fans, friends, or followers—will have an appreciable positive impact on your business.

In fact, there are many self-proclaimed business coaches who suggest raising your visibility as much as you can, believing (erroneously) that high visibility automatically leads to high profitability. These same people advocate what I call "fluffy marketing strategies"—things like constantly changing your profile picture, or your cover photo, or being photographed in cute dresses at the hottest parties—what I think of as the celebrity business model.

The celebrity business model can work for you if you are a celebrity, though even for celebrities, fame is short-lived. There is always someone newer, fresher, more dramatic who will come and usurp your place. Today's front page headliner is tomorrow's "what was her name again?"

And as for profitability? Don't even get me started. The celebrities who succeed in a sustainable way are ones who use their visibility for some other purpose. They use it to support their favorite causes or to fund additional businesses and side ventures. They plan and implement strategies for turning their visibility into dollars. This is why creating fame isn't enough—you must know how to utilize that fame to create money.

While it may seem like you should envy people who have amassed huge communities and followings, realize that there are some people online who have thousands and thousands of followers, but their businesses are not profitable. At the same time, while they have built these large online presences, they are getting really tired of giving out all their energy on the social networks and not seeing the results they desire.

Can I tell you a secret? Visibility still requires work to make a profit.

In my career, I've had the pleasure of working with some of the most well-known authors, speakers, consultants and coaches in business today. For each of my high profile clients, their communities easily numbered in the tens of thousands, and in some cases, in the hundreds of thousands. These are people you definitely know by name.

Yet, even for all their fame and reputation, they too had to sell like the rest of us. They had to make offers. They had to close sales. They had to provide service or follow up. Sure, in many cases, they have teams of people working for them who can handle all the details. The basic point is the same, however. Being well-known did not make money flow like rain; they still had to do the work. Of course, having more visibility can help you become more profitable, but only if you are making offers, closing sales, and providing service. If you have a model for monetizing your visibility, then your profitability should grow as your visibility does.

Visibility still requires work to make a profit.

All by itself though, visibility without conversion has little business value.

There is something seductive about people knowing your name. After all, getting attention is the first step to making anything happen. However, once you have attention, you must have some idea of how you will turn that attention into something useful for your business. You have to find a way to convert your visibility into dollars.

This is where most social media marketing plans have a missing piece. They focus mostly on visibility and getting attention, without a strategy for converting that attention into worth for the business.

I'm not suggesting that you socialize online solely for the purposes of business growth. Social media gives us a chance to meet new people, get new ideas, and can reduce the loneliness of working alone or working from home. At the same time, as a business owner, you must be aware of return on investment.

If you are investing in social networking without notable financial or relational gain in your business, then you are not receiving a good return on investment.

Without adequate return on investment, you can't afford to keep investing.

I'm not against large social networks. I'm only suggesting that you realize what you are building these large networks for—and if you don't have a large network yet—to think about why you really want one.

> **If you have a model for monetizing your visibility, then your profitability should grow as your visibility does.**

If you don't have a good business case for a large social network, it might be your vanity or ego talking rather than good business decision making.

In the work I do for clients, one concept we spend a lot of time on is the idea of "rightsizing" your marketing strategies to your business. Very often, there is a gap in what business owners think they need to do and what they actually need to do.

I see this when a new business owner comes to me and says, "I want your help in building my Facebook fan page to 1,000 fans." But when I inquire further, I find that she is looking to have a boutique business, offering highly-customized services. When I ask about how she sees Facebook fans as contributing to her business growth and profitability, most of the time I am met with silence.

This silence is one of my cues that she has taken on a goal which is not serving her business. If you are going to invest in something like building 1,000 Facebook fans, doesn't it make sense to know how this investment will serve your business as a whole?

Yet there is a pervasive sense that more and bigger is always the way to better. This is not true. It is far better, from a profitability standpoint, to have 10 clients paying you than 1,000 fans knowing of you.

But this is the missing link in most social media marketing. It is easy to be seduced by the platforms and all the lights and bells and whistles. Again, technology is only a tool. Remember, I said that all the social media sites and online marketing approaches are merely tools. And as tools, they need to be utilized in a thoughtful way for a desirable outcome.

All the social media technology in the world will not help your business if you have no clear strategy or plan.

When new potential clients come to work with me, our conversations often begin with a discussion of their current profitability and popularity in their business. To my way of thinking, profitability is how much money you make, while popularity is how many people you know who can help you make that money. I don't intend to sound like money is the only thing—certainly people derive many other satisfactions from their businesses. But what I see, often, is that people will chase popularity (measuring or noting how many friends, followers, fans they have) rather than examine their profitability (how many of those friends, followers, fans are actually purchasing regularly or even at all.)

You can't truly know how much influence you have with a group of people until you ask them to take action.

And if they aren't taking action, they aren't helping you become more profitable. If you start to assess how much of your online network actually engages with you regularly and responds when you ask them to take an action, you are very likely to see that the real number of people who are engaged and paying attention is much less than your total fan or follower base.

When you start to detect patterns between what marketing you do and what results you get, you start to know where to spend your time for the most impact.

Before we move on, I wanted to share a bit more about this concept of rightsizing your marketing.

When a new client comes to me, I always pay attention to a few key factors.

Initially, I take a look at what their desired business goals are, both in terms of money and time spent working. I try to assess for the realism of their goals and desired time frame, and I always try to assess if there is any urgency around money. Usually, if a client needs to make money quickly, they are most likely going to want to focus on tricks or techniques rather than big strategy. This isn't necessarily all bad, but there is always a sense of rush and urgency when people are reaching out in a last ditch effort. Yes, a cash flow crisis can happen to any of us, but if it keeps happening, there is something wrong with your business model or approach.

After looking at their goals and the realism of their time frames, I take a look at how far away they are from reaching their goals, with an eye to gauging what it would require for them to reach their goals. There is a fundamental difference in how much marketing you must do to fill two clients slots compared to fifteen.

Third, I take a look at the client's existing network and community. Very often, there are unused or hidden assets that we can tap to help create cash flow more quickly. If any data exists about recent past successes or conversion numbers, we look at those next. Then, finally, we put all these pieces together to create a plan of action for their online marketing.

While for most of my life I've always worked harder than necessary, I'm now a big fan of doing just enough activity to get the results you want. I like to know about how much effort it will take to reach my goals, and this is something I try to encourage my clients to think about as well. While there are no 100% guarantees in business, you can find some patterns to how your business tends to grow if you actively look to identify these patterns.

If you look at where your most recent four clients came from, for example, that is a pattern. Wherever they came to you from should be a place you cultivate for more clients. So, for instance, let's say that you got one new client by referral, one new client from your website, one new client from a teleseminar you hosted, and one new client from an in-person networking meeting.

If you just need four additional new clients, would it make sense to think that you might try to activate more referrals, maybe add some more content to your website, perhaps encourage more people to listen to your teleseminar replay, and also go to an in-person networking meeting?

When people come to me and say they need help with their marketing, I always want to understand if they don't know how to market or if they don't know how to read the clues that their past success has left for them.

All the social media technology in the world will not help your business if you have no clear strategy or plan.

In my experience, success leaves a breadcrumb trail. When a particular marketing strategy has brought you success, keep doing it until you find one that works better or suits you better. And similarly, if you have tried and failed, don't hang on too long trying to fix it. There are hundreds of ways to market your business. Why get bogged down with the ones that aren't working for you?

By following the clues of success and rightsizing your approach, you can reach your goals more quickly and with less effort. This helps you gain a growing sense of confidence in how much work you have to do in order to attract and sustain the size of business you want.

The simple focus on rightsizing your actions to meet your goals can reduce about 75% of the overwhelm, stress, and anxiety you feel when you look to launch a new program or service, or when you look to promote yourself more intentionally.

For some reason, it seems to be an automatic habit that most of my clients immediately think too big about what is needed and in the process of thinking of all that could be done, they get overwhelmed and paralyzed and in some cases, end up doing nothing.

In fact, I had a conversation earlier today with a client who wants to attract more one-to-one coaching clients. This client, Amanda*, wants to gain four more one-to-one coaching clients. She currently has four one-to-one clients and a combined network of about 4,500, which included her email newsletter list, and connections on Twitter, LinkedIn, and Facebook. Four more clients sounded very doable to me.

When I asked her how she'd like to enroll these clients, there was a small pause, and then she rattled off sixteen ways she thought she might get these four clients. She became pressured, a bit out of breath, and seemed to be feeling anxious.

When I asked why she was feeling pressured, she said that she had started to feel overloaded and overwhelmed by how much work she would have to do in order to fill these four coaching spaces.

So then I asked her, "What if you didn't need to do all of that? How would you feel then?" (Relief.)

I suggested to her that we focus on maybe two or three ways to get new clients. Since her personal network was of a decent size, and since she had clients already, I didn't think it would take more than a few strategies to help her fill her client slots.

Understanding that she would have fastest conversion (that is, people would sign up more easily and quickly) if we focused in on her existing clients and business, we developed a three-part strategy to get more clients. The first step was to reach out to her existing clients and mention that she would welcome referrals. The second step was to mention this in her next email newsletter issue. The third step was to offer coaching as an upsell to an existing training where she had already enrolled clients.

It seems simple when you read it here, but think about this in your own business. If you focus on clarifying your goals and then rightsizing your marketing efforts, you will be able to have the results you want with less strain. Anything that can make your business easier and more profitable is a worthwhile approach.

You have some choice in how you market your business.

This also goes for your online marketing efforts, too. I believe you do need to market your business online; that is true. And I believe you have some choice in how you do this. In my experience, most people can only sustain two or three marketing avenues in an ongoing way. This may be something like a newsletter, social media, blogging, and then speaking or networking.

For most immediate cash flow generation, your promotional strategy for your business should include a mix of direct contact (either via live, in-person speaking, teleseminars, or webinars), content and search engine marketing approaches (this would include blogging, newsletters, articles and guest posting), and social media.

Where most business owners run into difficulties is when they focus too heavily on the content/search activities (blogging, newsletters, articles) without enough direct contact opportunities.

Business owners also run into trouble with focusing too heavily on social networking (i.e., Twitter, LinkedIn, Facebook, Pinterest) without using social media to create direct contact opportunities.

When you need to generate cash flow quickly, always look to your existing clients first. See if there are additional services you can sell them or new services you can sell them. From there, go one circle out, and try to reactivate past clients or people who inquired about working with you but never followed through. From there, go one more circle out and see if your colleagues or joint venture partners can assist you in some way. From there, go one more circle out and look at joining in some kind of event or direct selling opportunity.

> **Build your business in a way that suits you.**

At the same time, it is wise to build up your content and content promotion, so that you can eventually benefit from better search engine ranking and clients who might find you through Internet search.

If you need to generate cash flow quickly, it always makes sense to start with your closest- in circle of contacts and work outward from there. Blogging is not a fast client acquisition strategy. But over time, you can build up a body of work that might attract clients.

And while we're on the subject of marketing avenues—better to have fewer strategies that you consistently use than ten marketing avenues you only use occasionally. Why support a blog on which you only post once per year? Or a newsletter that barely gets out at all? Or social media profiles on sixteen sites when you only ever login to Facebook?

When you have a lot of marketing channels like these that you aren't using regularly, I would suggest that you've gotten caught in the trap of thinking you have to have them—because everyone says so—without paying attention to whether you're actually using them to your greatest benefit.

Although it is minimal in terms of costs to host a blog—you can get self-hosted WordPress for free and your own hosting for a few dollars per month, I'm also suggesting that you pay attention to energetic cost. There is some energetic cost to you in having a blog that you don't update regularly and feel you should.

I know first-hand that blogging can be a fantastic marketing avenue—but only if you actually post content regularly and engage with the blogosphere. Otherwise, a stagnant blog could look worse than no blog at all.

I do suggest you take some time to review your existing marketing channels and note which ones you're actually using regularly to build your business. Focus more deeply on those; the rest are just distractions. You don't need to succumb to peer pressure about these anymore.

In essence, I'm suggesting that you can build your business in a way that suits you, selecting the best marketing strategies for you: the ones you like and that you are likely to sustain.

Stay focused on getting clients first and then on becoming more well-known. In fact, getting clients first can often help you become more well-known. And by serving your clients well, you build a strong and solid reputation for excellence which has more weight and value than the 500 online friends you've never met.

In summary, when there is a choice to be made between pursuing popularity or pursuing profitability, I always suggest seeking profitability first. Focus on building a solid financial base with a regular source of income. Hang out here for a while. Grow your skills and confidence. Build up a financial cushion.

Once you are regularly and reliably meeting your expenses and have created a financial cushion, then look at investing in the larger visibility play if that suits your business model and business goals.

Too many business owners get this order backwards, where they focus on building visibility without a clear pathway to monetize their visibility.

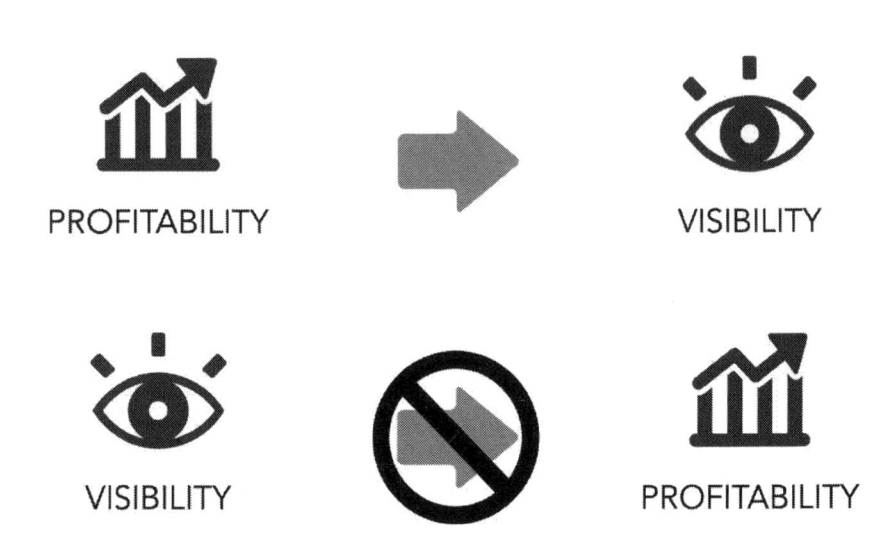

FIGURE 3-1: Profitability to visibility NOT visibility to profitability

Your business can survive without a ton of popularity. It cannot survive without enough profitability.

If I had to choose between them, I'd rather be less well-known and make lots more money.

How about you?

Chapter 4

WHAT YOU NEED FOR A MARKETING PLAN

IN ORDER TO develop a successful marketing plan, you must first understand what it is you desire to achieve.

If you're like most of us, what you desire to achieve will start off kind of vague and probably be feeling-based. You will be able to identify how you want your business to feel and most likely, at least a few specifics of what it will take to achieve these feelings.

So, for example, if I asked you right now what you wanted to achieve in the next year for your business, you'd probably say something along the lines of, "I want to help more people. I want to make more money. I want to take a vacation. I want to give more to charity."

If I were to ask you how achieving these goals would make you feel, you'd likely say, "Happy. Secure. Calm. Excited. Relieved." (And all other sorts of good feelings).

And, unfortunately, this is where most business planning actually stops. People identify what they want, perhaps identify how they want to feel, but don't actually take the next step, which is quantifying specifics of what they want to earn and how they will earn that money.

When I hear from a client that she wants to bring on four new clients, we immediately look at her resources for doing so. We craft a plan of action to meet her desired strategic goals. (We touched on this in an earlier chapter.)

Until you understand WHAT you want to achieve, you can't create a plan of HOW to achieve it. Once you have the WHAT and HOW, you need to decide by WHEN.

So the basic elements of business strategy would include knowing what you want to achieve, how you will achieve it, and by when you will take action in this direction.

While there are huge industries built up around business strategy, at the most basic level (and this level is profitable), the core mechanics of business are about connecting with enough people on a regular basis, selling them something at a profit, and retaining that relationship as long as it serves everyone involved.

That's it. That's the basic three-step process on which all business strategy rests. If you have these basics, you have the foundation of all that you need. Yes, there is always a way to make this more complicated, and there is always a way to make these business processes more efficient.

If your business is not growing as you would like, you can go back to these basic three steps and see where you need to make changes.

Are you not reaching enough people on a consistent basis? You need to market more effectively.

Are you not converting enough people into clients? You need to sell more often.

Are you not retaining clients long enough after the first set of sessions? You need to focus on client retention.

As I've already said, it's much more cost effective to retain a client than it is to search for a new one. So for most service businesses, we want to look at how we can retain clients for a longer period of time, thereby stabilizing our marketing and sales cycle into something with greater predictive value.

Let me give you an example from my business. When I first began my coaching business, I worked on a month-to-month basis, more or less. In retrospect, I did this for two reasons. First, it was a confidence issue—I wanted to know that the client had a way out if I wasn't giving them enough value. Second, I wanted a way out because I wasn't 100% committed to working with this group of clients ongoing.

In my experience, length of service offering directly ties to level of commitment- both from your client to you and from you to your client.

LEVEL OF COMMITMENT

LENGTH OF SERVICE

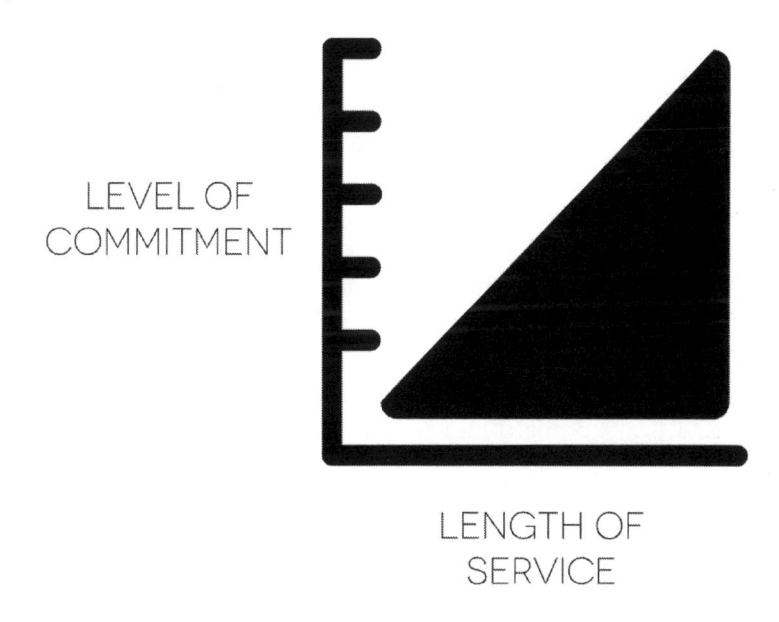

FIGURE 4-1: Length of service = Level of commitment

Also, length of service offering can enable you to smooth out the ups and downs of your income and business cycle.

So, I now offer service packages for six months at a time. I do this because I want to work with clients who are committed to me, and I want to have enough time and space to be committed to them. The content and search marketing work I do sometimes takes a few months to show results, so having a bit more space and cushion results in happier clients and less stress on me and my team. Also, a six month service cycle means I only need to enroll new clients about twice per year, and I can plan better for natural attrition and completion.

Yes, when a six month cycle is ending, there is a certain bumpiness in my income while renewals are being discussed and decided. But I manage this by staggering the start and end dates a little bit, so that client renewals are offset by a few weeks. This enables my business to provide deeper and better service to my clients because I'm not always so focused on getting new ones.

Does this make sense for you? Can you look at lengthening your service packages so you can spend less time marketing and more time in service delivery?

So step one of this process is to realize you need a strategy. Step two is to see where on the cycle of acquisition-service-retention you can improve.

If you find that you can improve your client acquisition—that is something that better marketing (online and offline) can help you with.

If you find you need to have more conversations that result in sales—that is something that sales coaching or business coaching can help you with.

If you find that you need to improve client satisfaction and results—that is something that training or education or experience can help you with.

If you find that you want your clients to stay longer in your business—that is something that lengthening your service packages can help with.

So when you are looking to build your marketing strategy, you want to first understand which part of this business cycle you are working within.

It is a mistake to try to correct more than one area at one time. Consider it a graduated process. You improve in one area which creates some challenges in the next; you improve the next and that creates challenges in the third, and so on.

Consider your business strategy as a kind of spiral, one that you'll revisit multiple times, but hopefully with new knowledge and confidence in each iteration.

Until you know what problem you are trying to solve, you won't know the right tools to use.

Before we move ahead, please take a moment to decide for yourself where your business could use a bit of strategic adjustment right now.

Do more people need to know of you? Then you need more tools for effective marketing.

Are you getting a lot of inquiries, but not making any sales? Then you need more tools for effective selling.

Are you feeling less than competent or confident in how you are serving your clients? Then you need more support, coaching, training, education, mentoring, or supervision.

Are you feeling that your clients keep leaving just as the work was getting really good? Then you need to look at ways to retain your clients longer.

There is one more level, a sort of pre-level, to this process and that is when your business is very new and you are trying to decide what to sell.

This pre-level can be baffling and painful. The best strategy I know for getting through this is to try many things and fail quickly. You will learn a lot more about yourself, your strengths, and what you like to do if you focus on finding out, as fast as possible, what you like and are good at.

You can spend 50 hours thinking about what you'd like to do, or 50 hours doing it. The 50 hours doing it will give you much more clarity, certainty, confidence, and real life data than you could ever have from 50 hours of thinking and research.

If you are stuck at this pre-level of what to do, this is something that a coach or mentor can perhaps help you with. You are not ready to create the rest of your business strategy yet, so this book may have to wait until this first question is answered.

If your business is in this early, pre-verbal stage and you could use some assistance in clarifying your next steps, I have two resources to recommend. The first resource is Lissa Boles (http://www.thesoulmap.com) who offers no-cost business advice in her SoulMapTV series, and offers an excellent paid class, The Callings Cycle, which can help you identify what is next for you. The second resource is Mark Silver and his team at http://www.heartofbusiness.com who offer an Organic Business Development coaching program that can help you uncover your "thing" and start offering it in the world. Learn more about both of these options and take action on the one which feels right to you.

If you know what you're offering and you've identified where you will begin making adjustments, now it's time to talk tools.

I think I've said this already, but it bears repeating here: tools are only to support the strategy. Tools are not a strategy.

With the rapid growth of social media, people have become caught up in this idea that tools equal strategy. They spend time learning all these little tips and tricks for using the various social sites, for instance, but they don't have a clear plan of what they want to achieve nor a way to measure what they are actually achieving.

I call this "spaghetti" marketing—where you throw a bunch of stuff out there to see what sticks. This is a possibly valuable approach initially, but online presence and credibility is built on consistency.

Remember how I said that people are looking for shortcuts—ways to make the best decisions they can with the least amount of effort? This applies to how they think about you and your business, too. They want to know what you offer, how you offer it, and be able to categorize you in some way so that they can make decisions about you faster.

What this means is that you can generate attention and visibility by delivering what people have come to expect from you. It doesn't mean that you're locked into doing things the same way forever, but it does mean that a certain level of consistency will create better results for you.

You don't have to commit to a marketing or business approach before you're ready, but once you commit to something, do it fully.

As I have said before, you don't need a blog just because everyone else has one. But if you decide to have one, maintain it. Use it. Let it create business value for you. Similarly, you don't need a newsletter just because everyone else has one. But if you are going to publish one, keep it as consistent as you can. Use the same structure. Send it out on a recognizable schedule. Stay focused on your core topic areas.

I know! I know! This is not the super creative and wildly juicy part of marketing. I get it. But the thing is this: reputation is built by consistency. People pay more attention to you when you deliver what they expect. This is why, for instance, in my business, I publish my email newsletter the same day and same time. I use the same format for every issue and keep the topic areas consistent. (If you wanted to get your own copy, you can do that by signing up at http://ProfitablePopularity.com/newsletter)

I rebelled against this for a long time, feeling like this kind of structure stifled my creativity. This was a mistake. If I had been consistent about publishing my newsletter from the time I first started my business, I'm certain that my business growth would have been more stabilized and I'd probably be further ahead of where I am now.

That being said, the lack of structure helped me realize that structure is very important. I see now that my email newsletter is a way of building relationships with my readers, and like any important relationship in my life, I don't leave it to chance. I don't call sometimes and not call other times. I don't say I will do something and not do it. I made a commitment, and I show up to do my part.

Be in an adult relationship with your business.

It's the same way with the other marketing I do. I try to decide what kind of relationship I can maintain with these marketing avenues (such as blogging, article writing, guest posting, speaking) and I build these into my regular working life. I know that I need to find ways to keep up with these commitments even when everything feels too busy and there is a lot going on.

This is when technology and automation can be very useful and where you learn how to stay with the plan even when it's difficult.

This is part of being in an adult relationship with your business—not throwing it over for the whims of your emotions. If you look at how you treat the important relationships in your life—perhaps the ones with your spouse or partner, children, family, friends—don't you show up to these relationships and do what you say you will? And don't you do this, even when it's sometimes difficult?

Why does your business deserve any less from you?

A worthwhile exercise is to take a few minutes and look at your marketing as an outside observer would. To this outside observer, would your business seem attractive? Do you seem to be consistent and reputable? Are you delivering on what you promise? Would this outside observer know what you do and how you do it? Could they feel reasonably confident that you would deliver what you promised?

Do the answers to these questions feel like yes or no?

If the answer feels like no in any of these areas, don't feel badly. We all have areas we can improve. Observing and identifying is the first step to making positive change.

OK. Now on to tools.

Once you've identified the part of your business strategy you need to improve (marketing, sales, service, retention), you're ready to take an inventory of your available toolsets to address the problem.

Let's start with the marketing toolset.

I'm always amazed by how many marketing avenues people know of and simultaneously how few they consistently apply. Many times, business owners feel they are bad at marketing, or they need to learn more marketing approaches. We all seem to feel some comfort in knowing 1,000 ways to promote our businesses, books, or blogs.

Though many people possess a lot of general knowledge about ways they COULD market their business, the actual consistent application of these marketing strategies is elusive. As I've already mentioned, most of us can be successful with just two or three marketing strategies that we use regularly. For some of you, that will be a relief. For others of you, that will feel untrue.

But please stay with me. If you are using two or three marketing strategies consistently and effectively, you can have a full service practice. Of course, if you have plans to build a larger

Use fewer tools to get more results.

network or platform, you might need to add a few others. But if we are first working on stabilizing your income flow, we only need two or three strategies to work for you to get your desired number of clients.

So the idea here is to use fewer tools to get more results. The marketing strategies you choose should be a mix of direct contact (teleseminars, webinars, in-person workshops, speaking, conferences, networking), content and search marketing (blogging, article writing, guest posting), and social networking (Twitter, LinkedIn, Facebook).

You will find that the most direct sales come from your direct contacts. This is because people have met you and liked you in person and this greatly reduces the barriers to them working with you. Content and search marketing work over time to build your reputation and thought leadership, which can eventually bring you clients. Social networking is good for immediate feedback and connection which can sometimes lead to new opportunities.

> You end up going around in circles, not really getting anything done, and not making any significant progress because you are not sure what problem you're trying to solve.

So if you look at your existing marketing avenues, which ones will you commit (or stay committed) to?

If you have committed to an area that isn't giving you the return on investment you'd hoped for, then this may be something you can address with mentoring, training, or coaching in this area. There is nothing stopping you from becoming an expert in each of your three chosen marketing areas.

If you are receiving many inquiries, but not making many sales, this suggests that your sales process needs some improvement. Learning more marketing strategies won't help you here. Learning how to have a successful sales conversation will. This does take practice, but the good news is that this is a very learnable skill.

If you are feeling a lack of confidence in your service delivery or what you're doing with clients, this is something you can address with mentoring, training, supervision or coaching. Reach out for the support you need in this area and make an investment in yourself this way.

If you are feeling that your clients leave your business too soon, you can look at how to improve client retention using various engagement and "stick" strategies. There are many ways to increase client retention starting from the beginning of the relationship.

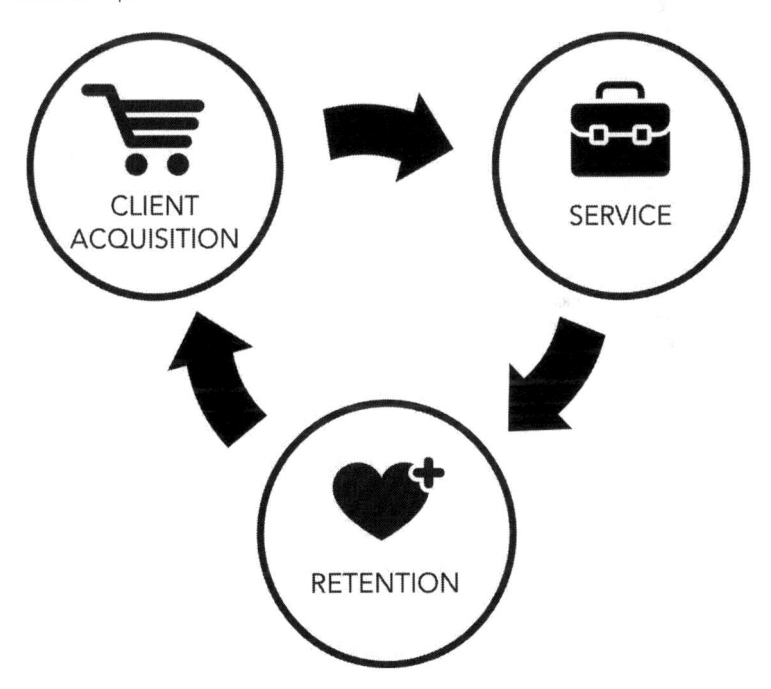

FIGURE 4-2: Cycle of client acquisition, service & retention

You can have improvements in all these areas of your business, but you probably can't have them all happening at the same time. And this is OK. Just start somewhere on this cycle, realizing that you'll probably revisit that place again a few more times as your business continues to evolve.

I often find that each step of business growth brings with it a new set of challenges and a chance to review or repeat our strategies in each of these key metaskill areas.

There is always room for improvement, and you'll become more agile with each of these areas the more you work with them. Growing your business is an iterative process. You'll return to the same kinds of concerns over and over again, though they are likely to differ in scope and scale as your business grows and matures.

Overall, the purpose of this chapter is to help you realize that you want to start by assessing what part(s) of your business need improvement then identify what the strategy is you'll use to improve them. Then you want to determine the correct toolset to address the identified problem.

Without this stepwise understanding, you end up going around in circles, not really getting anything done, and not making any significant progress because you are, essentially, not sure what problem you're trying to solve, and then, just as likely, you are using the wrong tools for the job.

The same way you wouldn't try to make a sandcastle without sand, nor would you use a hammer to put in a thumbtack, you don't want to operate your business from a place of trying to solve the wrong problem or use the wrong tools for your desired outcome.

Remember again, that more tools are not always better. You don't need to have 500 extra tools when three will do. You want the right tools, in the right proportions, to make your business strategy come to life.

When your business begins to flow more easily in the area in which you've made changes, it's then time to take another assessment and see what area needs attention next.

Chapter 5

CASH FLOW MAKES YOUR BUSINESS GO

IN THE WORK I do with clients, one of the main areas in which we focus is goal setting for cash flow.

Cash flow makes your business go. Without it, you can't easily invest in acquiring new clients, improving your infrastructure or business systems, or upleveling your skills.

Yet so often, cash flow seems to be the goal considered last, when it really should be the goal planned for first.

As I've shared already, your business has just three core functions: client acquisition, client service, client retention.

If you ask most entrepreneurs, they would agree that most of their focus is on attracting new clients (marketing) and at least to some degree, being hired by clients (sales). Fewer entrepreneurs focus on client retention, despite the fact that it costs 60% less to retain a client than it does to attract a new one.

Most businesses spend the bulk of their dollars and resources (time, energy, focus) on the process of attracting and selling to clients. You can save a great deal of money and time if you are able to retain your clients for a longer time period and if you are able to retain them and sell them more services.

There are seven main mistakes that can impede the gain and growth of cash flow in your business.

> **CASH FLOW MISTAKE #1**
> **Waiting too long to acquire your first client.**

This mistake refers to the experience of opening your business, but not making client acquisition a high enough priority. Instead, you spend your days fiddling with your website, designing your business cards, reading up on marketing, but not actually doing a lot of marketing.

So days and weeks go by, and sometimes months, and you are still waiting to work with your first client. In the meantime, your business expenses continue, and you may be spending a lot of money that you don't have.

> **CASH FLOW MISTAKE #2**
> **Believing you need huge infrastructure to attract your first clients.**

This mistake refers to the idea that you spend money on a website, and on business cards, and a separate phone line, and all these other business expenses because of the belief that you need huge infrastructure in place to attract your first clients.

I made this mistake when I first started my business. I felt I needed to have a very professional image, so I felt I couldn't begin to work with clients until my website was ready. At that time, I had more time than money, so I launched myself into learning how to build a website. By the time I finally got my website up,

I had learned how much I didn't know, and I began investing in infrastructure I had no use for. I would not advise this.

For most coaching, consulting, speaking, writing, or training businesses, you need less infrastructure than you think. Your fastest client acquisition avenues are going to be from direct client contact, so at most, you may need some business cards and a distinct phone line for your business. You just need something to give potential clients when they want to know more; you don't necessarily need a website with all the bells and whistles. For most new businesses, a simple website will do: one that identifies what you do, who you work with, and how to get in touch with you.

You can use your cell phone as your business phone or set up a free Google Voice line or an inexpensive Skype line to function as your business phone.

All you need to attract your first clients is an understanding of your service, an understanding of who you want to work with, a means to connect with them and have a conversation about working together, and a way to collect payment if you decide to move ahead. That's it. Just four things.

Once you have a few clients in your business, then you can look at building out infrastructure to grow.

One other area to assess as well is the area of your ongoing business expenses. Reducing your expenses can also lead to more available cash. I'm not speaking of reducing everything across the board, but rather, about being conscious where your money is going and clear about whether you are spending it in the most worthwhile places.

When I first began my business, I invested in the yearly lease of a telephone bridge line to hold teleclasses. I paid for this for almost a year before realizing two things. First, I was hardly holding any teleclasses, and so the line was sitting unused most of the time. Second, for my occasional use, I could probably be just as well served by signing up for a free bridgeline, or "pay as you go" option. This would give me access to a bridgeline if I wanted to have a teleclass, and it would also free me up from paying for one every month when I wasn't using it.

Similarly now, I make it a habit to review my business expenses once per quarter. I take a look at my ongoing subscriptions, software investments, phone lines, website expenses, and so on. I examine my largest expense areas by category and see if there is any place I can reduce my expenses going forward. I don't always find something, but often I do. Even though it may seem too small to worry about, spending even an extra $100 per month for a year means I've spent $1,200 in a place where I wasn't receiving value. $1,200 could buy a new computer, or could pay for some of my contractors, or could enable me to buy some new office equipment or something else which would make my business easier and better to run. At the end of the year, I want to feel good about where I've spent my money, and the best way I know to do that is by reviewing my expenses quarterly.

If you're not already taking part in a regular review of your business expenses, I'd like to suggest that you schedule this into your calendar now. Small expenses have a way of adding up, and why send out money where it isn't bringing you value?

> **CASH FLOW MISTAKE #3**
> **Not focusing enough on client service and retention.**

In my opinion, no matter the size of your business, you want to focus on excellent client service and look at how you will retain your clients after the initial agreement. In my business, I work with my clients in six month cycles, which means I only need to enroll new clients twice per year. Some other entrepreneurs I know work on a yearly cycle, so they only really need to enroll new clients once per year.

Cash flow generation is best when it occurs in a stable and routine fashion. When you know with certainty approximately how much money you'll be earning each month, you can better plan for your business expenses and business growth. You'll have money to work with if you want to hire a mentor or invest in more help.

Look at your current service offerings. How could you stabilize these into longer term sources of cash flow?

One way to do it, as I've already mentioned, is to look at offering your services in intervals of three, six, or 12 month cycles. If you are already offering your services in three month cycles, consider next offering these in four or six month cycles. Cultivating longer service terms serves several purposes. First, it enables you to focus more on client service and client retention because you don't need to be continuously enrolling new clients. Of course, you can always take more clients whenever you want, but the longer service term reduces your immediate need. It also enables you to work more deeply with your clients and to build stronger relationships. Often, longer service terms also enable you to create more results together, both as a function of time spent together and the trust within the relationship.

This longer service term can also help you learn more about your client's business and their needs, so you may be able to offer them more or additional services over time, which increases your profitability without too much additional effort.

The one downside of longer service terms is that if you enroll a group of clients initially within one month, your income may fluctuate when these clients all come up for renewal at the same time. For instance, if you enroll six clients for six months, in month six, you have a greater risk of income destabilization because six of your clients will be coming up for renewal.

You can reduce the impact of this in several ways. First, save some extra money to create a financial cushion. Second, look at offering incentives for early renewal. Third, perhaps stagger client start and end dates to reduce the "all-at-once" renewal effect. Fourth, seek to enroll at least one or two new clients each month, ongoing, so service terms all expire at different points. Fifth, provide really excellent service so a high percentage of your clients renew.

> **CASH FLOW MISTAKE #4**
> **Rushing to productize too early**

This mistake refers to taking your core business idea and turning it into a product too quickly, at the expense of continuing to offer the service directly. Good information products are worthwhile. However, it makes no sense to cut your main source of revenue in your business by commoditizing your knowledge into a product that people can buy for $197, $297, or even $497.

If you have a method that generates results, don't be too quick to turn it into an information product. Most people who buy your product won't use it. And if they use it, they may not use it well enough to get the results they could if they worked with you directly.

Productizing your knowledge too soon means that you've sold what you do too inexpensively, you've decreased the results people are obtaining from your method, and you've essentially cut off the upgrade path to sell them additional services.

This is not true in all cases, of course, but in many of the businesses I've seen, people feel too excited about turning their knowledge into a product, and they cannibalize their revenue in doing so.

> **CASH FLOW MISTAKE #5**
> **Not growing and nurturing your community between launches or using program launches as your only cash flow strategy.**

I've combined these together because they often occur together. This mistake describes an entrepreneur who is constantly launching programs or services, but the size of their available community is not large enough to support this frequent launch schedule.

Let's look at this one through a client example. I had a client, Grace*, who came to me because she was feeling overwhelmed by continuously offering her programs, but nobody was buying with any consistency. She had planned, essentially, a launch every other month, but was feeling overwhelmed and frustrated because her first three launches had only created two new clients.

She had been working this launch process for several months before she contacted me, and was stopped short when I asked her the size of her community when she began launching (about 400 people) and the size of her community now, months later (about 400 people).

She had not focused at all on reaching new people, and was, essentially, launching the same programs and services over and over again to people who had already been exposed to these offers and were not purchasing.

Yes, there is value in repetition, and yes, sometimes people will buy after they hear of a program enough times, but in general, it's a wise business strategy to focus on nurturing and growing your community in between launches so you reach more people on each launch. If you don't focus on growing your community, eventually you will not be able to sell anything because everyone who is interested has already purchased.

It is also wise to look at how you can reduce the number of launches you do in one year, so that you can focus deeply on fewer launches with better results.

**CASH FLOW MISTAKE #6
Inconsistency in your offers.**

This mistake, inconsistency in your offers, actually describes two types of errors. The first error occurs when you don't make sales offers consistently enough. That is, you don't keep a strong focus on making sales. You may sometimes offer coaching, sometimes not, or sometimes suggest people work with you or sometimes not. This inconsistency in when and how you make your offers will have a negative impact on your cash flow.

The second type of error occurs when you offer services just once or twice before moving to something new. This type of error seems to impact the bright and creative entrepreneurs the most, the ones who get bored easily and feel restless if they stay too long with an idea. This is a cash flow mistake because your reputation relies on you becoming known for something and being able to offer that "something" more than just once or twice.

The most stable businesses, cash flow-wise, are the ones that go deeply into offering the same menu of services, and when they find something that works, stay with it and don't leave it until they find something else that works better.

The discipline of maintaining consistency in your offers will help your cash flow.

> **CASH FLOW MISTAKE #7**
> **Generating cash flow without systems.**

This cash flow mistake tends to be one that more advanced entrepreneurs make. They come up with new ideas, launch them quickly, and because they often have cultivated large communities, they make sales. They rush to deliver the services they sold, and then move on to the next idea. The problem with this approach is that, often, there is a great deal of money that is left on the table.

Business systems are designed to support your revenue growth, but they only work if you use them. Examples of this mistake would include launching services or programs without a proper email sequence in place and without having a plan for evergreening this offer, creating new products rapidly, one right after the other, without taking time to develop a promotional and sales strategy for them, and so on.

Anytime you offer a program without a plan for keeping this cash flow going after the program is over, you run the risk of leaving behind some money you could have easily collected.

When you look at the programs and services you offer, look at what systems you could put in place to streamline the marketing, sales, and retention of those who purchase.

So, now that we've gone through cash flow mistakes, let's look at some positive ways to improve your cash flow.

First: Look to sell fewer items in your business, but sell more of them. So, for example, you might sell just three packages, instead of six. This will enable you to systematize your offerings, and then focus on selling more of the three packages.

Always go for simplicity in your offerings over complexity. Make it easy for people to understand and to purchase.

Focusing on selling fewer items also means that you can reduce your cost of client acquisition because you will be able to use and reuse marketing materials and created content, which will reduce your expenses of attracting new clients.

Second: Create complete and evergreen sales systems. What this means is that after you've launched and sold a program or type of service, look at how you can systematize it going forward so that it's easy to repeat this success.

Let's look at an example: Let's say that you offer a six-session training. You develop launch materials, perhaps do a preview call, and you get enrollments. As you move into providing the training, you might also want to convert your sales page to an opt-in page, so that you can begin to collect the names of people who may be interested to know when you next offer the same training. You can build follow up email sequences for those who've enrolled, so that you can guide them through the training, and perhaps, also, seed your next offer.

> **You take care of your business, and it will take care of you.**

If you invest the time in developing complete sales systems, including follow up and upsells, you can make more money more easily.

Third: Evolve your services and offerings to meet the needs of your ongoing clients. If you offer a program or service long enough, you will easily be able to see what other services you need to create or offer to meet the needs of your ongoing clients. Dig deeply enough into these areas so you are able to sell more of what people want.

I'll give you an example of this from my business. When I first began, I offered just one package: a full service online SEO package. While it met the needs of many people, it didn't meet the needs of everyone, but I was committed to selling more of fewer things, so I stayed with this one package. As I worked deeply with my first 15 clients, I began to see that a new service was needed: one that offered conversion tracking and cash flow consulting. I saw that while my clients were getting high rankings from the SEO work I did, many of them didn't understand how to utilize their new rankings to drive more revenue.

Until then, I hadn't given much thought to the possibility that my clients wouldn't know how to benefit from the SEO rankings they were pursuing, but once I understood this, I was able to add in some additional services to help address this need. These represented an evolution from my original offering, and my clients have been pleased with the change.

If you continue to generate worthwhile results for clients, there will often be at least a few new services you can offer them. Every new service you can provide to an existing client deepens the relationship and accelerates your profitability.

Cash flow isn't always easy, but it's usually not as difficult as people feel it to be.

The key is to find ways to generate income rapidly, and to keep this income flow going, even as you are exploring business systems, infrastructure, and so on. Never let the "non-income" producing activities of your day take up more time, space, and energy than the ones which are directly making you money.

Yes, of course, you'll sometimes want to keep tweaking the colors of your logo rather than having a sales conversation. But having the grit and self discipline to keep focused on cash flow, even when you'd rather be doing something else, is an indicator of being in an adult relationship with your business. You take care of it, and it will take care of you.

Create systems for your income generation. Try to standardize what must be done, so there is less effort required to generate a successful promotion. It's easier to create the base marketing plan and materials once, and then tweak/freshen.

In many cases, you must go slower than you think in order to make more money. There is usually more money in going deep rather than going broad.

When you are selling fewer things, you can better focus your energy to make a complete sales process, which to me looks like: course structure/offer, marketing materials, sales page, email sequence to make the sale, follow up sequence, and then maintenance sequence (i.e., opt-in page to be available between offers), and then a plan for client service/program delivery, and an upsell path (where will they go next?). See Figure 5:1 on page 88.

Yet too often, entrepreneurs do all the work of the first few steps (offer, marketing, sales) but don't do enough on the side of follow up, maintenance, and upsells. Always think about what your clients will need next and be consistent in offering it to them.

When examining various opportunities in your business, look first for the ones which you can see have the most direct path

```
COURSE STRUCTURE & OFFER
          ↓
    MARKETING MATERIALS
          ↓
         SALES PAGE
          ↓
       EMAIL SEQUENCE
          ↓
     FOLLOW UP SEQUENCE
          ↓
    MAINTENANCE SEQUENCE
          ↓
         UPSELL PATH
```

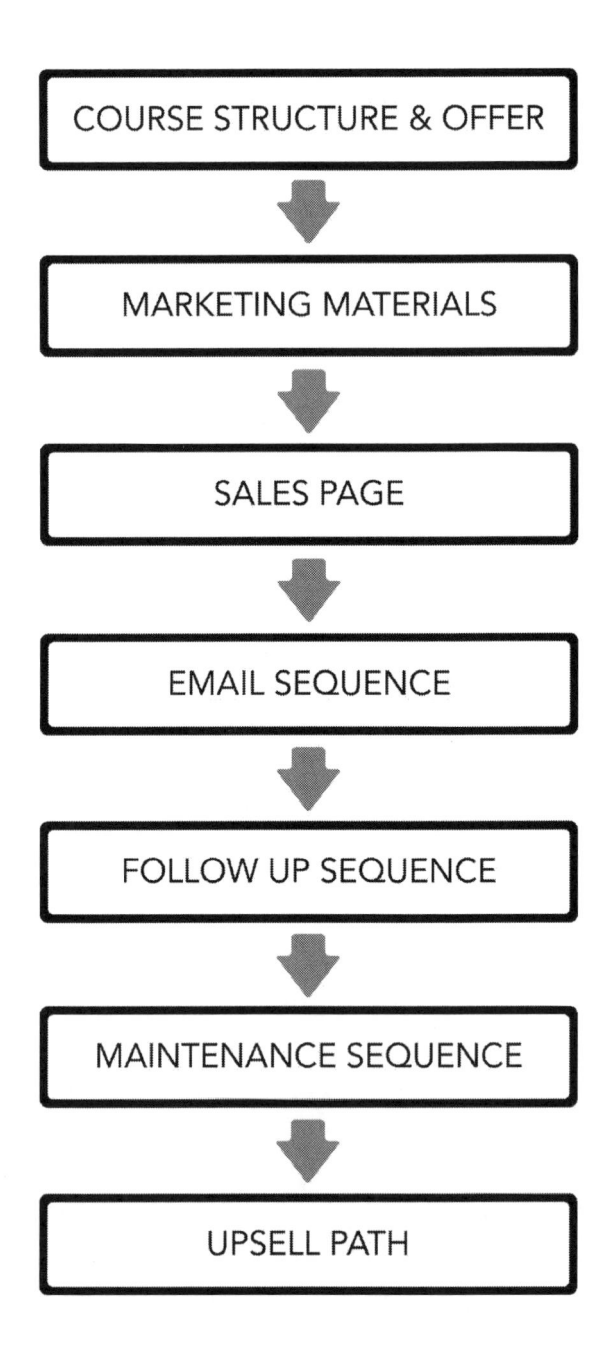

FIGURE 5:1: Complete sales process

to cash flow. This is vital if your business is in the early stages or needs more stabilization.

Focus on fulfilling the immediate cash flow needs of your business as your first priority each day, week, and month. Say yes to the most direct path to cash, and utilize your earned monies wisely.

When you adopt and live into the idea that "cash flow makes your business go," you'll be better able to determine where to invest your time and energy for the best returns.

NOTES

Chapter 6
CRITICAL THINKING IN YOUR BUSINESS

WHEN BUILDING YOUR business strategy, the importance of critical thinking can't be overstated, so I wanted to utilize this chapter to look at what critical thinking is, why you need it, and how to do it.

In my way of using the phrase, critical thinking about your business means that you exercise some combination of logic and facts to guide your business decisions. I believe that intuition is important as well, but you can't always have intuition on command. So while your feelings are important—and they do matter—they are not, by themselves, without logic, good indicators for what you need to focus on or do in your business.

Feelings aren't facts.

It doesn't mean that they don't give useful information. They do. It just means that you need to have some other markers or guidelines for making decisions when you are entering new territory or don't know what to do.

Having another gauge for your business decisions is especially helpful when your feelings seem weighted equally in two directions—meaning two options feel equally good. In these cases, your intuition may not be able to assist you in selecting the best way to proceed.

The thing about intuition is that it often speaks in symbols and metaphors. Sometimes, the meaning of these is crystal clear, without a doubt. Other times, the meaning is a bit obscured and somewhat blurry.

The voice of intuition is sometimes difficult to hear, and even when your intuition is prompting you to proceed a certain way, you still have to sift your intuitive promptings through some set of personal decision making filters in order to determine what, really, your intuition is directing you to do.

Developing critical thinking skills is one mechanism for putting together all the intuitive information you have, blended with facts and logic about your business, and using this resulting blended information to make better business decisions.

I can't emphasize this concept enough. We each need some kind of relevant and useful framework to use when thinking about our businesses. We need some structure that enables us to sift through equally good options to determine the best way to proceed.

As your visibility, reputation, and business grow, the daily complexity you experience will grow, too. And you'll find yourself making many decisions in a much shorter amount of time. Initially, this complexity may center around how to promote yourself and gain clients. From there, it may grow to encompass hiring people and managing them. After that, you might look to become a leader in your industry or to leave a legacy. Generally, as your business grows, you will experience more complexity on a daily basis.

If we take just one aspect of your business, growing your visibility on the Internet, you'll find that with growing visibility often comes much more opportunity. As you become more well-known, you'll naturally start to attract people who want to collaborate with you, who want to interview you, who want to hire you, and who want to invite you to speak at or sponsor their events.

In the first rush of this, you'll feel excited and want to accept them all. However, given the limits of time and space, you'll find, at some point, that you can't be in multiple places at once, that you are tired of flying across the country, and that you don't want to keep spending money to sponsor events you aren't even attending.

Sure, you can learn this through trial and error—no problem. But can you see the benefits of having some kind of lens through which to evaluate opportunities so that you can know better and more easily what to say yes to, what to say no to, and what to negotiate for in terms of changes? Without this lens, you won't really have a clear sense of how to move your business ahead in a sustainable and profitable way.

Let me try to illustrate this with a personal story. When I first started my first business, a psychology practice, I spent a lot of money. I invested in expensive Yellow Pages advertising and local newspaper ads. I began to dabble in online marketing but for the most part, was investing heavily in traditional, local advertising. Truthfully, I had jumped into having my own business with very little preparation or forethought, as a knee-jerk response to some significant betrayals by my then employer. In any case, I didn't know exactly what I was doing with regards to growing my business, but I ascribed to the idea—which I've now warned you about—that visibility leads directly to profitability.

Don't spend money you don't have to make money that never comes.

So, there I was with my very shiny and new business, spending money I didn't really have on promotions that weren't really working. Sure, I got some phone calls, but mostly from people who wanted to sell me more advertising. The trouble was, I didn't know how to decide if I should buy more advertising or not. After all, if visibility led to profitability, then it seemed like I should spend more to make more, right?

I wasn't 100% sold on this belief anymore, but I also knew I didn't want to be a quitter. So I continued to invest in local advertising and also began writing for a local business magazine. I began to get some interest and people reaching out to make connections, but again, very little business.

What I didn't know then was that writing for a business magazine was going to take a long time to gain clients for me because people only had contact with me once per issue, and the issues only came out once per month. I didn't understand that this process would take so long, so it looked like this wasn't working, either. Had I known to follow this writing up with perhaps a live presentation or in-person networking, these efforts might have brought results for me sooner.

I share this story with you for two reasons. First, to demonstrate that we all begin at a similar place. Unless we grew up in business, we all have to learn about business. Second, I want you to realize that knowing how to make business decisions is what ultimately determines your success. Without a proper foundation of knowing how to think about your business, you run the risk, as I did, of spending money I didn't have to generate money that never came.

So now that you see why I believe critical thinking is important, let's look at how to start to develop it and what benefits it has for you.

I want to open up the process of developing it by sharing part of an article I wrote for my blog[1] on this topic.

---

[1] http://ProfitablePopularity.com/blog

(Pay special attention to how I utilize this excerpt, as it demonstrates the concepts of repurposing and evergreening that we'll go over in the chapter of this book related to content creation and generation.)

Here's the article I wrote for my blog:

> Critical thinking is a dying capacity. Yet it is crucially important for your business.
>
> Simply defined, critical thinking is the capacity to examine and explore an idea from many perspectives, and after this careful consideration, drawing a conclusion based on facts.
>
> Wikipedia defines it as: **purposeful reflective judgment concerning what to believe or what to do.**
>
> There are several key elements to this definition.
>
> The first element is that **critical thinking is purposeful.** It is a behavior that is engaged in with intention and which leads to some outcomes or understanding. It is not to be confused with analysis paralysis, where you keep thinking and thinking and never come to a conclusion.
>
> The second element is that it is reflective. It is something you do **inside yourself**.
>
> The third element is that it involves some **decision process** about what to believe or what to do.
>
> Stated this way, it seems clear to me that critical thinking is an important component of business success.
>
> So, if critical thinking is so important, why does it seem that not so many people are doing it?
>
> I've noticed, over the past few weeks, that many of

my colleagues and some of my business acquaintances have been caught in what seems like endless loops of discussion, debate, and internal dialogue. They wonder, "Should I build a membership site?" or "Should I write an ebook?" "Do I put my prices on my website? Will that scare people off?" "Do I write to my blog two times a week or three?" And so on.

While all of these questions may be important, the difficulty with these questions is the answer to every question is both yes and no. **There is no one right answer.**

Additionally, the answer to these questions is not outside the questioner. They are not answers that someone else can give them about how to run and grow their business. People sometimes ask questions that have no answer and then spend a lot of time trying to find the answer to the question. This results in a lot of delayed activity and feelings of overwhelm.

At the heart of the questions, really, is a desire to have the best result for the least amount of effort. There is nothing inherently wrong about that, especially if a workable answer is easily forthcoming.

But when the answer is not easily obtainable, the answer is **not to sit and wait.**

The first step is to do some critical analysis of your options. Make a for/against list. Debate yourself on the pros and cons. Get some clarity on your own personal feelings of "Why yes?" or "Why no?" Put some facts to your feelings.

Then, when you've come up with a basic working plan, your next step is to take action—some action—in the direction that you think you might want to go. If you want to set up a membership site, start researching site options and pricing. If you want to write an ebook, jot down your outline. If you want to put prices on your website, go ahead and see if this makes any difference one way or another. Try writing to your blog twice a week and then three times a week and see what feels better to you and if the results differ.

In essence, what I'm suggesting is that you use **your business as your own personal critical thinking laboratory.** Press this button. Flip that lever. Do a crazy mad scientist kinda move. See what happens.

Our businesses want to evolve and grow, and the fastest way to do that is to **have an idea,** think about it long enough to **define next steps, take action** toward it, and then **adjust course** as needed.

(End blog post)

What I'm advocating here is a more curious, more exploratory approach to your business, and in that process of curious exploration, learning more about what is true for you. When you learn what is true for you, and how things work for you, you have taken the first steps to developing critical thinking for your business.

Remember how I mentioned the process of social decision making earlier in this book? That process where we want to make good decisions with less effort?

That applies here, too. Because we want to have the same results as other people with less effort, we invest in coaching, training, and mentoring to try to find a better and faster way.

That is wonderful and good, when it works. But at least 50% of the time, it doesn't work. That is, you invest in coaching, training, or mentoring to try to learn a system which you find either doesn't fit or doesn't work for you or both.

At the end, you feel badly. Either you are to blame because you're somehow limited or not good enough, or your mentor/coach/trainer somehow didn't deliver.

I believe that neither of these is true. Instead, what I believe is that you didn't consider critically enough what you were looking for, and your coach/mentor/trainer didn't push you to determine that.

When I invest in a coaching, mentoring, or training relationship, I always approach it as a successive approximation experience. What this means is that I never expect that it will work *exactly* the way for me as it did for the coach/mentor or even as it did for anyone else.

Instead, I expect that it will get me somewhat closer to my goal than I could do on my own. And how close it gets me is always a function of how accomplished that coach or mentor is at what I want to achieve.

It is impossible for anyone to teach you to be exactly like them. No matter how much money you spend, no matter how much you mimic or copy your mentor, you will never have the same results they had. The best you can achieve, in my opinion, is something close: better, worse, "gooder" or "badder," but close. Not exact.

When you see that other people are having more success than you are, remember, first, that we are very good at comparing our insides to other people's outsides. We live inside our skins, not theirs. We are very aware of our limitations and might not see theirs.

I do believe investing in training/mentoring/coaching is worthwhile. I do believe that success leaves clues: you can learn some important strategies or approaches by reading and learning from others who have been successful.

But the thing is, to me the heart of learning about the success of others is really about learning how to perceive or think differently for ourselves. Even if I were to try to exactly copy another person's success story (assuming I could even do this accurately or exactly), it is still very likely that I'd have a different outcome and experience. Mine might be worse, or it might be better, but it would, almost certainly, be different.

That realization of difference is what many people don't grasp when they invest in programs or products and try to follow the steps exactly.

Even assuming you could follow another person's success trajectory 100%, you'd still end up at a different place because you began as a different and unique person.

If you have invested a lot of money in learning programs and systems that either you never finished (I'm guilty of this!) or you've tried and they haven't worked for you, the goal of developing a more curious and exploratory approach is likely to be of huge benefit for you.

If you actively and consciously press this "here" to see what happens over "there," and do this often enough, you'll start to see patterns. Even if you read 1,000 stories of how other people have been successful, it won't have personal meaning, resonance, or relevancy until you actually start testing out their theories and approaches for yourself. You also won't know exactly how it applies to your business because their stories are just words on paper, not experiments you've gathered personal data on.

When we look at how ideas are created, we see that all ideas follow a three-step process of discovery as shown in Figure 6:1 on page 100 which can happen through accident or serendipity, experimentation, which usually begins with trial and error to identify what works, and synthesis, where we bring everything that works into a cohesive whole.

Yet too many business owners conceive of their business ideas in a kind of vacuum. They sound good on paper, look perfect to the eye, seem like they should work—but actually don't.

When this happens, you, as a business owner, have two choices. You can beat yourself up, or you can say, "Oh, good!"

FIGURE 6:1:
Three step process of discovery

(DISCOVERY → EXPERIMENT → SYNTHESIS)

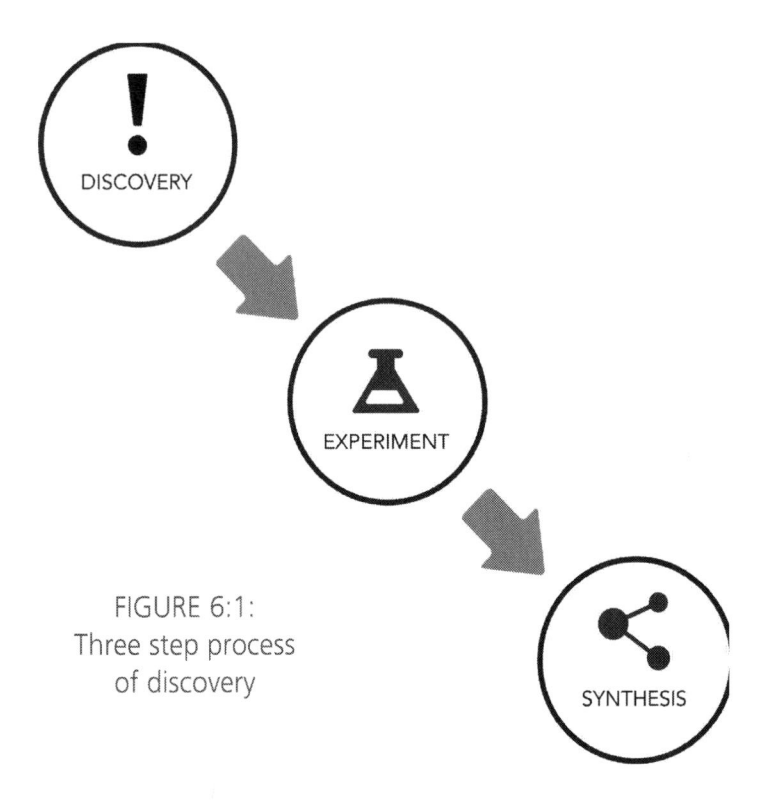

Being wrong is OK in business. It's better to not know and seek to learn, than it is to be so certain of your ideas and not be able to change your mind even when you really, really need to.

I see our businesses as a type of crucible. Every time we have a challenge in our personal lives, we'll see the same kind of issue in our business. If you have difficulty setting boundaries at home, you will have difficulty setting boundaries in your business. If you have trouble asserting yourself in your personal relationships, you'll have trouble asserting yourself in your business.

The good news about that is when you learn how to set boundaries or speak up either at home or in business, the new good habits tend to generalize and you're better at it everywhere.

I raise this because I feel that there is this huge pressure on us to have the answers, to have things figured out, and to somehow understand and know more than we possibly can.

This is why information is so seductive: we accrue more and more of it because we fear being caught short or being left behind. Information has no meaning in your business until you try it out, see what works, and turn information into implementation.

There is also a limit to how much information we can consume at any time, hence the term "information overload." Our brains are not wired to accrue masses and masses of information without having some structure or framework to utilize it.

In fact, the two means by which we learn new information, assimilation and accommodation, both rely on creating links between pieces of information and learning how to put new information into categories. So we are always only able to learn new things by understanding how they connect to what we already know.

My belief is that creating these connections is a very active process and one that can only be accelerated and confirmed by real life experience. We all learn faster when we have an idea and implement it, and then review the outcomes to determine whether we should continue with our plans or backup and try again.

This is how you develop critical thinking about your business. And this process of critical thinking, seeing what your business needs distinct from how you feel, and trying to understand the inherent pattern or process by which your business is growing and evolving—this skill of critical thinking is crucial for entrepreneurs.

If you're currently working on some perplexing problem, remember that the first stage of critical thinking is curious exploration.

When you develop a process of curious exploration in your business, you'll develop confidence and a sense of how to think about your business in a way that is right for you. You won't lose days and weeks and months agonizing over decisions that have no one right answer. You'll be able to engineer small tests for yourself, so that you can take the next steps and gather data to help you decide and move ahead.

Every business challenge is meant only to help you become more agile—to gain a new way of seeing and responding that you didn't have access to before. The greater your willingness to test and experiment, the faster you'll gain in agility and the less time you'll spend feeling overwhelmed, confused, or paralyzed.

One thing Andrea J. Lee (http://www.WealthyThoughtLeader.com) once told me which I always remember is this: "In business, if you're wondering about something and you don't know how to answer, it's because you haven't asked enough questions yet." This applies whether you are thinking about pricing, services, packages, work hours, anything. If you don't know how you will answer the question, it means you need to ask more questions, and gather some evidence and data. The longer I am in business, the more I believe this to be true.

I see, more than ever, that I can only rely on successive approximations, gathering my own data, comparing it to the pathway discovered by others, and ultimately, coming to my own conclusions and decisions. And once I come to my own conclusions, that I take notable and meaningful actions on the knowledge I have gained.

In this way, I have a good sense of the "lay of the land"—my business's distinct topography—and I can start to build a repository of data and experiences to help me guide my business forward with greater confidence and a more skilled hand.

I want the same for you.

Will critical thinking solve all your business problems? Perhaps not—but it can solve many of them. At the very least, it will give you a chance to flex your mental muscles on interesting problems, ones that are new and challenging as opposed to boring problems, ones that keep showing up the same way all the time.

And for me, give me new and interesting over same and boring any day.

Chapter 7
BUSINESS CLARITY

ANOTHER KEY BUSINESS foundation is around business clarity—finding it and keeping it.

Have you ever felt confused in your business, like you weren't sure what to do? Maybe you weren't even sure how you felt, and worse, couldn't seem to figure that out either?

We can't take action until we know how we feel. Sometimes we need some tools to help us uncover how we feel.

In my experience, anxiety and fear can sometimes cloud us, making us take rash action to avoid desperate circumstances. In times like these, it's so wise and worthwhile to quiet our fear and anxiety long enough to get clear on what we want to do.

Clarity comes first, and then we apply critical thinking on top of it.

Just in case you, like me, sometimes have trouble finding clarity in your business, I wanted to share some ideas on going from unclear to more clear.

Having clarity in your business can be, sometimes, one of the most challenging aspects of running your business. Should you do this? Or that? Now? Or later?

Do you spend money to make money? Or should you save your money for a better opportunity? What if you have too many clients? What if you don't have enough?

And so on. Combine these questions with an increased rate of information flowing into our lives each and every day, and this is the perfect combination for confusion, overwhelm, and frustration.

Having been in business now for just over 14 years, and having changed my business several times during those years, I have developed five strategies for finding clarity when I need to make an important business decision and am not sure what to do.

I am happy to share these five strategies with you, but first, let's do a little bit of groundwork/foundational work to help make sure you're asking the right questions.

ASKING THE RIGHT QUESTIONS

Asking the right questions is the first stage—a foundational stage—of gaining clarity. The right question is the one that is the most important, most relevant, and—this is key—the one that will help you move forward and take action once a decision has been made.

My educational background and training is in clinical psychology, and I have thousands of hours of experience in providing psychotherapeutic services. Through this lens, I see that many people seek therapy when they have gotten stuck in asking what I would consider to be the "not-right" questions. I don't believe any question is actually ever wrong, but I do believe that there are some questions which are more right than others, especially if you are looking to make a decision and act on it.

The idea of the "not-right" question is one I use myself to

determine if I am looking in the right place to find an answer. Examples of "not-right" questions are ones where the answer is not knowable and where knowing the answer—whatever it is—won't actually help you take action.

In romantic relationships, examples of "not-right" questions, in my opinion, might be ones like, "Why couldn't she love me?" or "Why did he treat me that way?" Knowing the answers to these questions may or may not help you. And even if you knew the answer, the answer would not lead immediately to action. So you find out that "she" had a bad childhood. OK, so what? Or that "he" is commitment-phobic and doesn't want to settle down. OK, so what?

Knowing this information may help you understand the situation better, but knowing this information alone is unlikely to help you take action.

So, similarly, in your business, you are likely to ask yourself questions like, "Should I choose rounded corners for my business card or not?" Unless you have a strong preference or reason one way or the other, the answer to these questions won't get you closer to making a decision.

If instead, you ask "Do I like rounded corners better than straight corners on my business card?" you have an answerable question: a yes or a no.

Asking the right questions relies on focusing on what's most important, relevant, and meaningful. And this, inherently, suggests that you don't want to spend too much time on questions which aren't likely to make a meaningful difference or lead to action.

The other element of asking the right questions is in how you ask them. Try to avoid "Yes" or "No" questions in your business as much as possible. You rarely want to start there, unless you're already sure and comfortable with your decision.

But if you're not as clear, better to start with clarifying questions to help you decide your way to "yes" or "no."

CLARIFYING QUESTIONS

Clarifying questions, as they sound, are questions which help shape and define the problem in a more useful way. They help put scope and framework—parameters—around the question so you can be sure you're considering the question in the most meaningful way.

So, for example, a clarifying question might be something like, "What makes "X" a good option?" and then, "What makes "Y" a good option?" You'll need to explain and explore more about each possibility to answer the question.

Another type of clarifying question puts parameters around the problem—such as Who? What? Why? Where? When? How?

Examples of these types of questions would be:

- Whose responsibility is this?
- What needs to be done?
- Why am I considering this? What am I trying to achieve?
- Where can I make the most difference?
- By when must I decide?
- How will my decision be implemented?

And so on.

The literature on creativity states that we actually come up with more creative decisions when we have two limits or two parameters around our thinking. So, rather than trying to consider all possible alternatives at one time, consider placing two restrictions on the question as a means of shaping the solutions.

For example, in my business, I was recently working on developing a new service package. I found myself feeling initially confused because I had kind of thrown in all these possible combinations and had no way to make choices between them.

Once I put parameters in—"What service package would give the most value to the client at the least expense to me?"—I was able to more easily sort and discard options that wouldn't work. Since I provide done-for-you marketing services, I must always be aware of the best balance of client satisfaction and cost management—and so, these are often my two restrictive parameters.

Similarly, when considering new strategies to add, I run them through these two filters as well, and keep only those that make the cut.

Putting parameters around your questions will help you get clarity.

> **What service package would give the most value to the client at the least expense to me?**

WHAT WILL HELP YOU ACT

The final element of the foundation is to know what will help you act—that is, how will you know when you've come up with a workable solution?

For some entrepreneurs, they will feel a sense of relief or calm. Others will feel a sense of excitement. And still others will feel like they can exhale and take action.

Knowing your own personal cue for when you've landed on the right decision is an important element to have in place.

Now, on to the five strategies:

5 STRATEGIES FOR FINDING CLARITY

Once you have the right question, your restrictions, and the way in which you'll know you've come to the right answer for yourself, it's time to try these five strategies for finding clarity.

My suggestion is to try one, and see if that works. Give it a day, and then try another and so on. If you try all of these at once you are likely to feel just as muddled and no clearer.

Strategy #1

Talk with a close friend or colleague. This might sound overly simple, but it works. If you take the time to explain your dilemma to another person, this can be useful in helping you clarify what's important and what's not. Your friend or colleague can offer you new ideas or perspectives, or simply, just be an empathic ear. Sometimes, the nature of having to explain to another person helps us see something we were missing.

> **ACTION STEP**
>
> Create a list of 3-5 people you can be in touch with for empathic listening and advice when you need. And be ready to do the same for them, if asked.

Strategy #2

Make a pros/cons list. When you have asked yourself an open-ended question about the challenge you're facing, a simple pros/cons list can be helpful in weighing your alternatives. I suggest you actually take the time to write this out on a piece of paper or type it into the computer, rather than just keeping the two lists side by side in your head. Make a list of all the benefits of one solution and all the downsides of that same solution. Repeat for each possible solution. Sometimes, these lists can help you see, sharply and clearly, what option offers the most pros and the fewest cons.

If a simple pros/cons list doesn't work, you might try a weighted one. The first step is the same: make the list of benefits and downsides. The second step is to "weight" each item in your benefit list as +1, +2, +3, and each item in your downside list as -1, -2, -3, with -3 being more negative than the -1. Once you've done this weighting, add all the numbers together. You'll be able to see which solution is the best, given your specific concerns.

Let me give you an example, a true one from my business.

When I was sitting down to write this book, it was coming at the end of a very busy and exhausting year. I really wanted to write this book, and I was also thinking that it might be nice to rest a while before tackling another project. Since you're reading this book, you know how this turns out, but here is the weighted pros and cons list I made to help me decide.

Pros to writing the book now:
- ✓ I really want to (+5)
- ✓ I think it will be a good book and will be useful (+5)
- ✓ I think it will help me build my reputation and visibility (+4)
- ✓ I believe it will help me attract clients (+4)

Now, notice that I weighted more heavily the things I was pretty sure about, that is about really wanting to and thinking the book would be useful. I wasn't as sure about the other two, but I thought they were reasonable possibilities. This is why they received a slightly lower number value.

Cons to writing the book now:
- ✗ I'm tired and could benefit from some down time (-5)
- ✗ It feels like a lot of work to write a book and publish it (-3)

And so, if you add up my pluses (from the Pro group), they total 18 (5+5+4+4). If you total my minuses (from the Con group), they total -8 (-5-3). So, my weighted list leans +10, which is the difference of the Pros minus the Cons.

So I wrote the book.

> **ACTION STEP**
> If you have a business question right now, make a pros/cons list. See if that helps you find clarity.

Strategy #3

Toss a coin. Now, I don't mean to sound like your business decisions aren't important, but the idea of tossing a coin is a good one—and I'll explain why in a moment. To implement this strategy, assign one outcome as "heads" and the other outcome as "tails" and toss the coin. Whichever side of the coin lands face up, that's the option to pursue.

Now, as I said, it might seem funny to use a coin to help you make a decision, but I think this quote explains it best:

"When you have to make a hard decision, flip a coin. Why? Because when that coin is in the air, you suddenly know what you're hoping for."

> **ACTION STEP**
>
> If you've spoken with a trusted friend or colleague, and also made a pros/cons list, now is a good time to flip a coin. What are you hoping for?

Strategy #4

Look to the past. If you have been in business any amount of time, you probably have had some success, actions which have worked well for you before. If you are feeling stuck around a decision, it can be wise to revisit what worked well for you before and to see how you can repeat that success in this current situation.

So let's say, for example, that you want to attract more clients. You review how you have attracted clients in the past, and realize that you once had three really good clients who came out of a networking meeting you attended. Given your past success in this venue, and presuming, to start, that nothing has changed, probably attending another networking event is a worthwhile action to consider.

Success leaves clues, and sometimes revisiting what worked in the past is a wonderful way to move ahead.

> **ACTION STEP**
>
> Review some areas of past success. Generate a list of what worked in these situations. See where you can take similar actions now.

Strategy #5

Look to the future. Sometimes, we can't make new decisions using old data. There comes a time when we might want to step out into new, uncharted territory, and we can't do that by looking behind us. So the fifth, and final strategy, is to look out into the future, and ask yourself, "Which of these options feels the most how I'd like to feel?" and "Which of these options is most likely to help me get where I want to go?" or even more simply, "Which option feels the best to me right now?"

We each have a sense of intuition and wisdom that guides us when we really aren't sure. We sometimes can't hear this sense because we've too frenzied or nervous or anxious. But if we get silent, become still, and engage in activities of the body—eating good food, taking long naps, spending time in Nature, we will, very often, find the answers we seek.

In writing out these strategies, I considered putting this step as the first one, since it's always a good idea to start from ourselves. But on reflection, I decided to put it here, as the fifth strategy because it represents to me the homecoming—a way of returning to ourselves, after we've tried all the other strategies.

While it is unlikely that you'll be faced with paramount business decisions of incredible depth on a regular basis—and I do believe that most business challenges can be resolved using strategies #1 - #4—I do think there might be times where some deeper soul-searching is required, and a sense of where you want to go is needed.

In these times, the best approach is to be gentle with yourself. Take care of your physical body and nourish it fully, with rest, good food, relaxation and play. Each of these activities will help reduce your worry and stress and can open the pathway for your subconscious mind to take over. It's no accident that we often come upon great solutions when we've stopped worrying about finding them—when our minds and bodies are engaged in other things.

Being still and patient with this process can be difficult, but the outcomes are always worth it. Decisions and choices you make from this place of calm knowing often carry huge weight and can keep you going when times are difficult.

ACTION STEP

If you've tried strategies #1 - #4, and still feel unclear, it's time for some radical self care. Take yourself out to lunch. Watch funny movies. Read good books. Spend much time in Nature. Journal. Laugh.

The answer will show up. That's a promise.

And there you have it: three foundational pieces plus five strategies to help you find clarity.

When you need them, they are here for you.

I hope you put them to good use.

Chapter 8
BUSINESS RESILIENCE IS VITAL

ONE OTHER CONCEPT I wanted to touch on as being critical for business success is the concept of business resilience.

When I was writing my book, Overcome Rejection, The SMART Way, one of the foundational thinking pieces in my coaching business, I was interested in identifying some strategies people could use to both protect themselves from rejection and to better manage rejection when it did happen.

I used the term "rejection" in that book, but I've since refined my thinking some and now see it as related to resilience. Rejection is the experience of being rejected; resilience is the process by which we can keep ourselves intact, happy, and whole even after we've been criticized or rejected.

I think this is an important topic to discuss because in some way, rejection—fear of it or recovery from it—shows up in business too.

I know, from my own life and that of my clients, that without having a certain amount of resilience in your business, you run the risk of being overwhelmed by your negative emotions and stuck in terms of how to move ahead.

This is especially worse if you have a very sharp internal critic and if you struggle a lot with feeling like you need to fit in, when you really want to stand out.

A sharp internal critic combined with fear about what other people will say is one of the most potent anti-action combinations there is (she says from the vantage point of all too familiar and uncomfortable experience).

Although this has been an area that I have experienced a lot of challenges with, I think that these challenges have given me some perspective on how to become more resilient and to keep growing myself and my business even when I have felt afraid.

The concept of business resilience is one that is very timely as our world becomes more and more uncertain.

Let's look into this concept more deeply.

One way of viewing resilience is as a continuum where one end of the continuum is about showing up fully, and the other end is about feeling shameful, constricted, or somehow collapsed.

The truth is, from my years of work as a psychologist, that we all struggle with the "dark" end of this continuum—the ashamed, collapsed place. We have all felt this way at some point, or we feel this way within certain areas of our lives.

We might be professionally successful and show up fully at work, but struggle with poor intimate relationships and struggle in shame in private.

We all have arenas where we show up fully, and we have arenas that make us shrink.

The only difference is that some people acknowledge it and try to work with it, and others don't. Your degree of shame and resilience is directly tied to several factors in your life. The good news is that resilience can be bolstered and grown; the bad news is when you don't realize this is the case, and you keep suffering when you don't have to.

This whole concept of business resilience might seem a bit strange to include in a book on business and marketing. The way it makes sense to me is that you can't become as well-known and successful as you want to be if you are spending too much time on the "shame/collapsed/constricted" end of the spectrum. If the bulk of your life energy and personal resources are being spent in trying to manage your internal critic, win the approval of others, and to fit in, you have many fewer resources to expend on being courageous, experimental, and innovative.

It may also be that your own capacity to overcome and be resilient in the face of obstacles is a core part of the value you bring to clients, and so it would serve you and them well to integrate it.

If you look at your personal reserve in terms of a point system, you can see what I mean. Let's say that each of us has 100 points to meet the demands and responsibilities of our lives. If you are spending 80% of your "points" in keeping yourself safe, trying to convince yourself that you aren't that stupid and in trying to make sure everyone else is happy even if you're not happy, you only have 20% of your "points" available to complete all the other tasks of your life.

Contrast that to a person who spends 20% of their points tending to their internal critic and negative self talk but then has 80% available to achieve their goals and do what they want to do. In this example, it's not difficult to understand that the more we can quell our energy drains and the feelings that shame and overwhelm us, the more resources we can bring to achieving our goals and creating results we want.

I believe the concept of business resilience is one that deserves more attention than it gets. You cannot grow a bigger business until you have grown bigger yourself. Each challenge you face in business is a personal one. Whatever negative feelings shut you down in your personal life are going to be the same negative feelings that shut you down in your business and vice versa.

To slightly adjust a famous quote: "We're not entrepreneurs having a human experience. We're humans having an entrepreneurial experience."

This means that the experience of being human will always be the first brushstroke that paints our experience of being entrepreneurs.

However we are as humans will be how we are as entrepreneurs.

I see the process of growing our business resilience as one way we can learn to relate to and interact with the uncertainty of business. There will always be things we don't know, and there will always be outcomes we fear.

But if we are able to keep ourselves grounded and steady, and to find ways to keep proceeding with our plans, even when we feel small, afraid, squinchy or overwhelmed, we are much more likely to reach the goals we've defined for ourselves.

The concept of business resilience has inherent in it the idea that when we are resilient, we keep showing up to do what must be done. Especially if we're afraid, or we don't want to.

When we contemplate building a larger business, whether larger means making more money, having more impact, becoming more well-known, or some combination of these, we must overcome our fear of stepping out into a bigger spotlight and taking our place on a bigger stage.

We risk experiencing criticism when we dare to stand out. How we manage that criticism, if it comes, is based solely on how well we've cultivated resilience practices up until that point.

CHAPTER 8

WHAT KIND OF PRACTICES CAN MAKE US MORE RESILIENT?

1 Recognize where you feel vulnerable.

Recognizing places where we are personally vulnerable or where we quickly collapse into shame. Knowing what this feels like when it happens.

I had an experience once where I accidentally cited a statistic incorrectly during a speaking presentation. One audience member quickly spoke up and began berating me about my mistake. Statistics are not one of my strongest areas, and I quickly became overwhelmed and very ashamed. This was made worse by the fact that I was on stage in front of 150 people. The thing I knew was that I wasn't going to be able to talk my way out of this using my intellect which was my first inclination. The first thing I did was notice how I felt—really overwhelmed, collapsed, and stressed. My heart was pounding and I felt like I might cry.

So what did I do? I acknowledged the audience member and thanked him for raising the error. I laughed and said that this was one reason why I studied psychology and not math. And that if the rest of the audience agreed, I'd like to be "let off the hook" for this mistake, and be able to share with them the rest of the information I'd come to present.

And here is what was interesting. I found that by admitting my error, trying to use humor to alleviate the tension, and finding a way to bring the audience back to the main focus of my presentation, it helped me to view this situation differently. I didn't feel as upset when it was over as I thought I would have, and I didn't need to relive it over and over for days after.

The unexpected gift? I received rousing applause from the audience, and several of the members came up to me afterward, thanking me for making light of my mistake and showing them that it was okay to make a mistake like this—even in public—and keep moving ahead anyway.

This led me to conclude that what we do in the first few seconds of experiencing rejection and criticism has the power to influence how quickly we bounce back from it. In this case, I don't think I could have come up with a way to handle it if I didn't first let myself feel how badly I felt. I needed to feel that first, without shrinking, avoiding, or collapsing, in order to find a way to manage the situation effectively.

Once I managed it this way, I had this experience in my toolkit to be able to refer to again, if I ever needed it.

So we must first recognize how we personally feel and experience vulnerable situations.

2 Build a strong support network.

The funny thing about shame is that it can't be healed until it is witnessed compassionately by another. Left to ourselves, we can sit in the roiling whirlpool of our shame, unable to get out and in danger of drowning. But when we can share our story with someone else, someone who cares for us and who can be compassionate to us, we can find a place of more compassion for ourselves. Nothing worthwhile and lasting can be built without some level of support from people who will keep us moving forward when we feel like turning and running.

3 Practicing good self care.

OK. I know, I know. But it is really, really, really true. We can't bring the best to our businesses if we're not sleeping well, not eating well, not relaxing, and not finding time for play, creativity, and renewal. We need time to turn our brains off, and we need space to build in meaningful practices that are not about the pursuit of fame or wealth.

We need to be careful that we don't get caught in a process of constantly running ourselves ragged and being too exhausted to enjoy our achievements. Where is the fun in that?

4. Decreasing negative self talk.

Did you know that most of us have a thread of conversation running within ourselves all the time? And that 80% of what we say to ourselves is negative?

Yikes.

5. Increasing our integrity

Increasing our integrity means that we intentionally and actively create a greater alignment between what we say and what we do. It means a greater "match" between what we say is important and the behaviors we exhibit.

Ongoing misalignment between what we say and what we do drains us of energy. Any energy drain is a trigger for reduced resilience.

6. Creating a reserve

Instead of running really close to your limits, try living with a bit of reserve. This can be reserves of time, energy, focus, and also money.

When you live with some reserve in these areas, you generate a sense of spaciousness in your life and business. This spaciousness leaves room to create more positive feelings and more positive outcomes.

One thing I began doing this year which has been really fun is keeping track of all the good things that happen in my life and business.

I have a medium-size, wooden box, and in there, I place a small slip of paper with the date and the event each time something good happens in my life or business.

You can think of this like an appreciation box, where I gather events that I notice and appreciate and value. Some of my slips of paper mark occasions like signing a new client or being interviewed for a major media publication. Some mark working less, without feeling guilty. Some mark client gains or successes that I am a part of.

I enjoy seeing the box filling each week. Sometimes, I go through the slips of paper and remind myself of how much good is happening. This never fails to make me happier or even to cheer me up when I am in a bad mood.

The idea with all of these techniques is to shift our thinking from what is broken to what is going right. We want to move forward with as much personal reserve as we can, and the best way I know to do that is to care for our bodies, souls, and spirits, to build strong relationships, and then, from that full and satisfied place, build our businesses.

All of these suggestions are designed to help us cultivate our own sense of self and sense of groundedness and to be able to hear the voice of our intuition as it speaks to us. Only when we make space to be wise, can we grow our businesses with vision and wisdom.

Chapter 9
BECOMING A CATEGORY OF ONE

WHEN I THINK about the concept of profitable popularity, I think of this as being present when there are frequent client inquiries, stability in your business income, and a sense of optimism and hope about your business, aided by strong business relationships and good social engagement, and new opportunities flowing to you.

When both the financial and social sides of your business are running well, you're in the ultimate sweet spot to grow your business and make a larger impact.

Of course, the exact numbers of dollars and friends/fans you seek will be determined by your individual business goals.

But one of the fastest ways I've seen to reach profitable popularity is to become very distinct in yourself and what you offer, and therefore become a category of one.

If you've heard of the concept of "blue ocean strategy," this is essentially the same idea. You want to disrupt the existing marketspace and carve out your place as distinctively as you can.

You will know you've achieved this when you have new clients approaching you regularly and when new clients feel they must work with you, with no delay or hesitation.

It really is true that the more you stand out, the more people can see you and want what you offer. You still have to complete the sales process with these people, as I've already mentioned, but you can gauge how distinct you currently are by how you are attracting clients and how you are making sales.

For example, if you look at all the business services available today, you'll see a lot of overlap. All the marketing consultants/coaches are promising you strategies to attract more clients. All the sales trainers are promising you strategies to make more sales. All the SEO folks are promising you top search engine rankings. All the social media gurus are promising you big money from social media.

So, in a sense, the actual results of a business service are not, by themselves, unique. Most everyone in a particular segment is promising a similar most-desirable outcome.

Therefore, promising the same outcome isn't going to be a category-defining strategy. You will have to evaluate your process or method to find what makes you distinct. And if you've ever had clients before, there is something that makes you stand out from others. To become a category of one, you have to try to explain what this is, and find a compelling way to share this with others. We'll talk more about building your know-like-trust factor in a later chapter, but for now, let's just open up the thought process around what you do that's the same as everyone else, and more importantly, what you do that's different from everyone else.

The biggest challenge in this process is in staying with it long enough to actually determine what truly makes you unique. And what is unique is determined not just by you, but also by the other businesses offering your same kind of service.

Here's what I mean.

If you run a retail store that sells women's clothing, you're competing with all the other women's clothiers out there. You might start defining your category by saying, "Well, we stay open longer hours than everyone else." OK, this might be a benefit, or it might be incidental. You then ask yourself, "How does staying open longer matter to our customer?" The answer is that it may not. So that might not be the correct foundation to build your category upon.

But let's say that you own a women's clothing shop that specializes in clothing for women who have had mastectomies. You can promise customized, thoughtful service, along with wonderful clothes that make post-mastectomy women feel beautiful in their bodies and confident again.

Now, yes, if all you sell is post-mastectomy clothes, you might feel that this is easy to understand. What, though, do you do if your post-mastectomy clothes are only a small part of your inventory, and you actually sell many other kinds of clothes as well?

Many coaches, consultants, healers run into this kind of question for their service businesses. They feel hesitant and worried about branding on just one focused aspect because they feel they will be turning away business by doing so.

The thought pattern is totally understandable and common as this is one of the biggest reasons people avoid claiming a niche. My experience, and that of my clients, shows that first claiming a niche is a valuable and worthwhile step in creating your own business category.

You've heard this before, I'm sure, but a niche is not something you select once and stay with for the rest of your life. It can and will evolve. But selecting one small slice to focus on initially can help reduce the feelings of stress and overwhelm and give you a place to focus as far as building your business.

It also enables you to hone or sharpen a particular skill set, so you can more rapidly build expertise in this particular area.

> **Just because you called yourself something and put it on your business card doesn't make it more true.**

We'll go over more about why specific expertise is important in an upcoming chapter, but for now, please realize that I'm suggesting you become an expert in a particular area in order to build your confidence and cash flow.

While we're on this concept of the "category of one," I also want to suggest that you avoid spending a lot of money in branding yourself to this category until you are sure you like this focus and can make money from it.

We humans are funny creatures in that we detest uncertainty and will often spend a lot of money, time, and resources in declarations before we've actually tested them out and see if they work. I'm thinking about people who have uncovered a potential business distinction, and the next day, brand themselves with this, redoing their website, logos, business cards, and headshots before they've even tested this idea in the marketplace and seen any results.

Just because you called yourself something and put it on your business card doesn't make it more true. You will have much better results overall if you are willing to test and experiment with your ideas before committing your resources to them fully.

In my experience, most people, myself included, go through about three or four possible categories before they find one they can settle into. Therefore, it doesn't make sense to invest so fully in branding each of your interim categories, as that can lead to big expenses and confusion, both for yourself and your market.

So how do you begin to uncover what makes you distinct in your service category?

There are basically two ways that I know of. The first involves an exploration of what you want to be known for; the second involves an exploration of what is actually attracting clients. When both of these align, there is an almost magical "click." When they don't line up quite right, this can be confusing and difficult.

I hope that giving you an example from my own business will help. As you may know, one aspect of my business involves offering search engine ranking and visitor generation services. I've helped build traffic and influence for many kinds of businesses, using many kinds of strategies. Yet I have always felt I wasn't really only a search engine optimization (SEO) firm. I offer social media marketing, but wasn't really a social media marketing firm. I offer business coaching, but wasn't only a business coaching service, and so on. I had a sense that my business was sitting at the intersection points of various business services, and so actually defining what my business is has been difficult. I sat in the question for many years with no clear answer. Through this whole time, I was exploring new pathways and gaining new skills, gaining real life data about what clients were asking for and willing to pay for.

As you might expect, I first tried adopting standard labels for my business. "I run a marketing company. I run an SEO firm. I run a social media company." And so on. Even as I was saying this, I realized that none of these were distinct enough, not even fully accurate.

Running a marketing company didn't really tell people anything. Marketing is vague, and always, to me, has this sense of promotion without a focus on sales. Since I care very deeply about my client's profitability and business earnings, "running a marketing company" didn't really capture the breadth of what I do. "Running an SEO company" wasn't quite right, either, as SEO is just one part of the larger framework and strategy. There was more to what I offered and was offering than just simply search engine ranking. I also help my clients with metrics and tracking, and I help them sell more from the traffic they are getting. So "running an SEO company" wasn't a large enough container either. The same kind of problem arose when I used the term "running a social media company." The fact was none of these were large enough containers to encompass the full range of what I do and like to do with clients, but I didn't have a name for it, and so I was using whatever seemed more commonly understood.

It took quite a bit of time—years, in fact—for me to gather all the pieces together into my current business and to feel like this container was large enough to encompass all that I like and want to do.

What I finally understood is that I am in the business of profitability. My overall desire and goal for my clients is to help them find ways to make more money more easily. This is my big picture desire and my big why.

The tools I use to assist with this are search engine optimization, social media marketing, traffic tracking, and conversion. I also use my background in psychology and my understanding of human dynamics to help my clients create profitable popularity.

It took me years to realize this. Going through all the years of "not knowing" was difficult—I seemed to be going all over the place with no clear path. I delved very deeply into topic areas, but then moved on from them very quickly as well. I changed my business focus several times in my anxious quest to feel like I was making decisions and doing something—anything! In retrospect, I now see that I was "trying on" various types of businesses and testing my business ideas, seeing what I really liked and what actually stuck.

At the time, as I said, it felt confusing and like I had no idea what I was doing. Yet I can look back and see that each year I invested in this way has had significant positive impact on my business now. In creating a narrative about my work history and experiences, I've been able to connect the dots, and see how everything from before was leading me here.

And I'm pretty sure that, no matter where you are in this process of becoming a category of one, there will come a time when it all makes sense and where everything comes together. Until then, I'd definitely recommend following your joy and the breadcrumb trail of success clues. It's totally fine to seek out experiences that make no conscious sense or which seem weird. Just be sure to make an active effort to integrate these experiences in the realm of logic as well. What did you learn from this experience? How will it help you build the business you want? Is it something you should repeat?

What I finally understood is that I am in the business of profitability.

By doing this, you're essentially putting some framework around your experience, so that you can create a pattern or narrative about where the intersection is between what you like to do and what other people are looking for.

The best way to find this intersection is with real life data. You can read all the books and theories, hear stories of how other people did it, but you can't know for yourself if it will satisfy you until you take action and test your ideas.

While this process can be vague and might sometimes feel uncomfortable, the benefits are worth it. What I've seen, in my own experience and that of my clients, is that when you take the time to define precisely what you do, in the language of what your clients will willingly pay for, you build your business more easily.

If you wanted to start exploring your own personal framework for becoming a category of one, I would invite you to complete this next exercise.

CATEGORY OF ONE

Take a piece of blank white paper. On that paper, create three columns. In the first, list the names of your most favorite clients. In the second, list what you helped them with. In the third, list what you most liked about this work. Do this for at least 5 clients; 10 clients would be better.

Then, after completing the list, leave it for a few hours and come back to it later.

When you come back to it, review the second column, the one in which you listed what you helped these clients with. Mark with an asterisk* or star the items which appear more than one time. Most likely, you will have some overlap in the areas you work within.

Repeat this process for the third column, marking with an asterisk* or star the items which appear more than one time. Again, you most likely will have some overlap in the areas you most enjoyed.

Now, take the starred items from both columns and used them to complete this sentence:

> The kinds of concerns I help people with are _____, _____, _____ (filling in the starred items from column #2) and what I enjoy about this work is _____, _____, _____ (filling in the starred items from column #3).

After completing this, you'll have a statement which reads something like:

> "I help people who are shy, anxious and worried. What I enjoy about this work is how they become more confident and calmer and better able to reach their goals."

OR

> "I help people organize their life experiences to write their life stories and what I enjoy about this work is seeing their pride and helping them build their legacy."

So you see, this statement actually fulfills the first part of the category of one—the part where you define what you would like to be known for. Presumably, if these are your favorite clients, and you've selected the work you enjoyed doing with them, you will want to be known for this.

So that is the first part. The second part is whether clients will pay for this. The quick answer is Yes. If you've been paid before, you can be paid again.

But the bigger question is not, perhaps, whether you can be paid, but rather, how much you should be paid. This is tied directly to your level of expertise at creating the outcomes you say you can create.

This is why, early on, I suggested that you start small and improve your skills in a notable way. I recommend this for two reasons. First, because it builds your personal confidence in the work you do, and second, because people will invest more to work with you as an expert.

If you can help create desirable outcomes for people, and you can do it in some way that is easier, faster, or better, people will invest to work with you. Depending on the results you help create, people might be willing to invest a lot to work with you.

The key to standing out is to provide notable value in a particular way and to do it easier, faster, or better than anyone else in your marketspace.

Once you become a category of one, you will often be the first person people think of and their first choice for who they want to work with.

Becoming a category of one improves your profitability because it keeps you from being commoditized based on price—meaning people don't necessarily have a direct way to compare you to anyone else because there isn't, by definition of being a category of one, anyone else like you.

The more you differentiate yourself, the higher the fees you can charge. And of course, the higher the fees you charge, presuming your costs remain the same, the more profit you make.

Sometimes people worry about stepping out and defining themselves so distinctly. This is not just because they feel this limits their choices and options (such as when people rebel against choosing a niche or area of specialized focus), but also because people sometimes don't want to experience the risks of standing out.

Sometimes it feels easier to fit in than it does to take a bolder, more visible stance. Yet I think that taking a bold stand for what you believe in is important, both for yourself, and to provide a clear beacon to those who are looking to you for leadership and guidance.

Consider yourself like a lighthouse, standing resolute on the beach, calling forward all the "ships" who are seeking shelter in your harbor.

It sounds a little bit dorky, maybe, but the image is a solid one. If the lighthouse is uncertain, wavering its light, turning on, turning off, the ships trying to navigate by it will become confused. If the lighthouse keeps moving its position, let's say it could move around and be at one point on the beach and then out on a sandbar, can you imagine how that would mess up all the vessels trying to navigate by its light?

They may get lost on the way to harbor, or they may never make it there at all.

This metaphor is one to really sit with. Think about how you are with your clients: are you a lighthouse with firm foundation and a steady light? Or are you a little bit blinky (which might also translate to ambivalent or confused)?

How you answer that question in your deepest self will have a huge impact on whether you are the person you need to be to have the business that you want. Very often, to have a bigger business, we have to grow a bigger self.

We have to be better at defining what we do—what is us, and what is not us. We have to be better at communicating this to others—what we will do, and what we won't do. We have to be better at navigating our own uncertainty when it arises. We have to be disciplined to deliver on what we promise.

In many cases, this requires that we grow up in some key and fundamental ways. As you may know, I'm a psychologist by training. Due to this, I can't help but see our insides and our outsides as very interconnected.

When I used to provide psychotherapy, I was always aware of how well aligned my clients were. I knew that when clients were aligned, that is, when their insides matched their outsides, they experienced much better outcomes and felt happier and more at peace. The really wonderful thing was that a change made anywhere in their lives could, eventually, generalize to all parts of their lives.

For example, if a client had difficulty setting boundaries at work, we could help him or her practice setting better boundaries at home first. Eventually, the boundary-setting skills would generalize—they would move from the sphere of home to the sphere of work. So, ultimately, the client solved his problem at work by strengthening his skills in the safer practice environment of home.

This process of skill set generalization also applies to entrepreneurs. (After all, we're people first, right?)

The way I see it play out in business is this: the same limitations you have as a person are the same ones that will play out in your business.

For example, let's say that you have difficulty saying "No." That difficulty will play out in both your personal life and business life until you make a change. Until you make that change, your business will have a certain size and a certain configuration.

Once you make the change—learning how to say No—your business's size and configuration will change. You can see it as your business evolving as you do.

So if you don't yet have the confidence or expertise to become a category of one, realize that your internal foundation may need some attention so that you can truly step into the brilliance of your full self, and create a unique and remarkable business that you can feel proud of and truly own.

Isn't that what you want?

Chapter 10
THE SEVEN SOCIAL CURRENCIES OF ONLINE MARKETING

THE ONLINE WORLD represents a type of social economy, which contains seven main types of social currency: attention, engagement, reputation, being known, being liked, being trusted, and being talked about.

Each currency is distinct and separate, just like pennies are distinct from nickels, and nickels from dimes, and so on. Yet all group together to make up the category of currency.

Your business building strategies can all be defined by gains and losses in these forms of social currency as truly as they can be defined by gains and losses in physical currency.

When your business is high in physical currency (cash flow) and high in social currency (attention, engagement, trust, word of mouth), you are operating in the best of all circumstances in terms of profitability and popularity.

While I'm not an economist by any stretch of the imagination, I do think it's useful to have a larger metaphor from which to view our online participation.

One comparison that works well for me is to think of our online relationships as being guided by an exchange of social capital.

Social capital is a term coined by 16th century French sociologist, Pierre Bourdieu, who saw each individual as residing in a particular social space, one that could be made larger or smaller by the types of capital articulated through their social relations.

In more direct terms, what this means is that people's social standing is enhanced, or diminished by the sum total of social currencies they express through their social space.

I see some parallels between Bourdieu's theories and the world of online marketing. One example is in the idea of your website's "neighborhoods." This refers to the process of where your website resides online. This isn't about your physical domain name or hosting, but rather, what sites your site links to and where it receives links from. Your site's ranking and authority can rise and fall based on the flow of this kind of social currency through your site.

Link out from your website to another respected and reputable site and your site gains by association. Even better, have a respected and reputable site link to you, and your site gains even more by this connection. In essence, some of the value and "goodness" (also known as link juice) transfer from the first site to the one it is linking to. This is why it is important to place your website in good company and to keep this relationship strong and growing.

You can see this phenomenon at play in social networking and in joint ventures, too. Social networking (connecting through sites like Facebook, Twitter, and LinkedIn) is all about currencies gained, traded, and shared.

If I make a funny post on Facebook (and I sometimes do), my gain in social currency can be measured in how many "likes" and comments that post receives. When people have taken time to read my post, "like" or comment, they have, in essence, given me some of their attention, no matter how brief, transferring some of their social currency to me.

As you know, the posts which get a lot of likes and comments tend to be more active—the initial social exchange can accelerate additional social exchange.

And then, of course, there is the anticipated return or reciprocation of the attention. If someone perpetually "likes" your Facebook updates, you probably feel, at some point, that you should return the favor, at least checking out their page and profile and finding something to "like" back. We all seem to do this quite naturally, understanding the concept of trading attention and engagement back and forth.

Let's continue with the example of content on Facebook, so you can see how each type of currency gets activated in this platform.

As I said, when someone pauses in their newsfeed to read your update, they have given you their attention. That's one form of currency.

If they "like," comment, or share, they have participated in engagement, the second form of social currency.

If you can engage enough people enough of the time, you begin to accrue the third type of currency, which is reputation. People begin to expect that you will continue to provide updates of value, so they are more likely to continue to pay attention and engage. Your reputation grows.

As your reputation grows, you become more well-known—the fourth type of social currency. As more people come to know and interact with you, they are more likely to like you—the fifth type of currency. And finally, when they know and like you, they are more likely to trust you—the sixth type of currency.

When they know, like, and trust you, they are likely to begin to tell others about you, or refer others to you—this is the seventh type of currency, word of mouth.

```
ATTENTION
   ↓
ENGAGEMENT
   ↓
REPUTATION
   ↓
KNOW
   ↓
LIKE
   ↓
TRUST
   ↓
WORD OF MOUTH
```

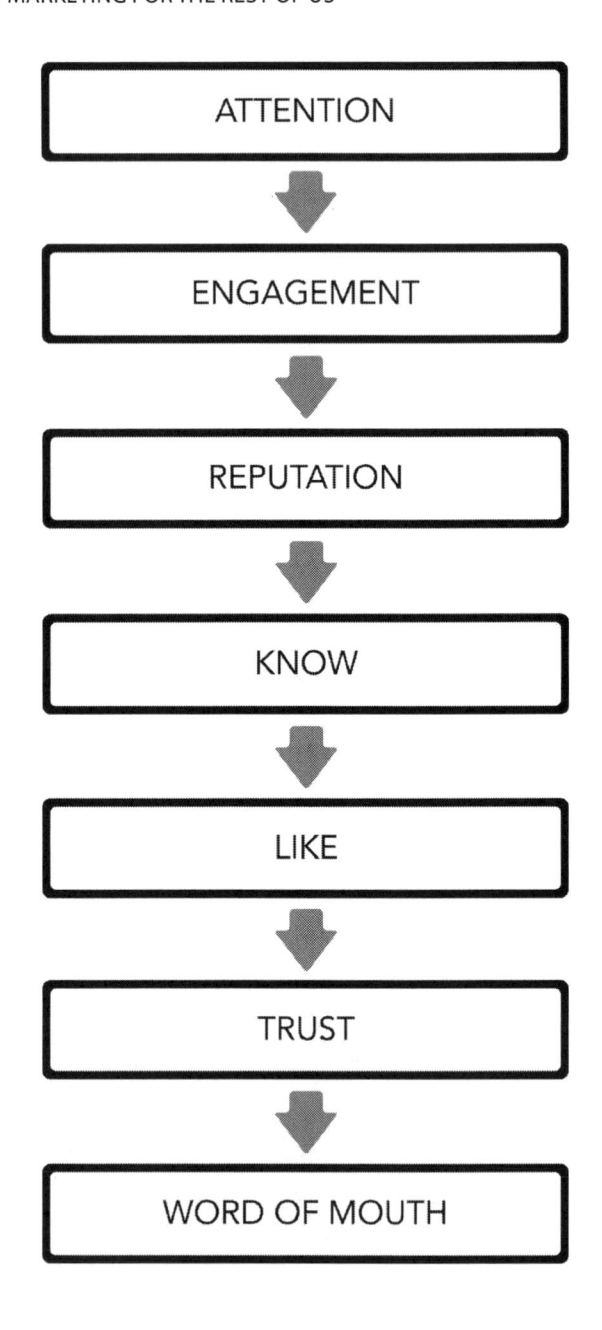

FIGURE 10:1: The seven types of social currency

You can build a reserve of these types of social currencies, similar to how you might save money in a bank. You can continually provide good and relevant content, and you will see your social capital grow. To the extent you focus on building real value and shared connections, you will be able to activate these seven social currencies to your benefit.

When you have built a reserve of these social currencies, you can effect changes within other people's social spaces as well. If you endorse them from your position of high currency, they are likely to receive more attention and engagement right away. If they manage this well, they too can build their reputations and become known, liked, and trusted—and maybe even talked about.

It is also possible for this to work in a negative sense. If you break trust, for instance, people will begin to shift their social currency away from you. They will reduce their attention and engagement, thus reducing your reputation, and so on.

I see these seven currencies as being crucial to online success, and they must be applied in a strategic and thoughtful way as you invest time on the Internet.

When you are looking to build your presence and popularity online, there are certain techniques you can adopt to accelerate the speed at which you attract fans, friends, and followers. These are based in basic human psychology and transfer well to the online world. We'll go through these one by one.

Before we do that, however, I want to take a few minutes to discuss the concept of 1,000 true fans. This term, coined by Kevin Kelly,[2] refers to the idea that a business can reach a six-figure income simply by cultivating 1,000 true fans. Kevin developed this model for musical bands, saying that if one band could create 1,000 true fans, each of whom spent $100 per year supporting the band (such as through buying music, attending concerts,

---

[2] kk.org

purchasing t-shirts, etc.), this band could easily make $100,000 in one year.

This model has implications for those of us building our businesses, too. In this model, a true fan is someone who provides you both social currency (attention, engagement, they know you, like you, trust you, and maybe even tell others about you) and they provide physical currency (in the form of real dollars spent with you). It speaks to the idea that having 1,000 true fans—people who will talk about you, and spend with you—is better than having 10,000 "non-true" fans—people who will talk about you, but are unlikely to ever invest with you.

This is where, in my opinion, most marketing goes wrong. It focuses almost exclusively on the idea that greater visibility automatically confers greater profitability. And while that would be easy and so great if it were true, it doesn't work that way.

There are many examples of people who have amassed large followings online, who have generated big numbers of fans, friends, followers, but these people are not making enough money. Their visibility is not automatically translating into cash flow.

Your popularity must be tied to sales in order to be profitable. By itself, popularity does not create cash flow.

The shift to make here is moving from thinking about fans/friends or followers to true fans.

If you're just starting out, what will it take for you to activate your first 1,000 true fans?

If you already have 1,000 true fans maybe you want to see how you can activate your next 1,000 true fans, so you have 2,000 true fans. Then, from there, you might activate 3,000 more, so you have 5,000 true fans, and then double that for 10,000 and so on.

Most of us can conceive of cultivating ultimately 1,000 people who know of us and buy from us.

You may not need that many people to reach your income goals. You may not want a business that is that large. That's ok. The key idea is to make the shift into making 1,000 profitable connections over the course of your business. Or, if you'd like to reach a seven-figure business, realize that you only need 10,000 true fans. Either way, this becomes a more discernible goal.

If you do this over a ten year period, you only have to consistently make 100 connections per year. If you want to do it more quickly, you might make 200 connections per year.

The shift...is that you're moving from millions reached to thousands influenced.

The value in this exercise is it gives you a framework for understanding how many people know of you compared to how many people are buying from you. Then you can look at how you can actually increase your number of true fans to get to the magical number of 1,000. Or, if you're already at 1,000, how can you increase it to the next, most important increment?

The shift here that you're making is that you're moving from millions reached to thousands influenced. That's so important because with the microfragmentation that's been accelerated by social media, by the fact that people are becoming in some ways more and more difficult to group into any particular demographic or psychographic, we really are not looking to reach millions of people. You're looking to influence a certain group of people. When you are planning your promotional campaigns or your marketing campaigns, I would encourage you to not just go for volume or not just go for reach, but to actually look at how many of those people you can meaningfully connect with in whatever way so that you can actually start to build influence with them.

The metrics are shifting from purely a numbers basis to how many people are actually taking action. That's the shift from millions reached to thousands influenced.

So the first key point is that we each want to be cultivating true fans. The second key point is that we likely need fewer than we think to reach our income goals.

Most of us are selling services and products that we offer for more than $100 dollars. If you had 1,000 fans, and were reliably selling $500 of goods or services to each of them once each year, you'd be earning $500,000 from these 1,000 relationships.

> The metrics are shifting from purely a numbers basis to how many people are actually taking action.

Now, of course, it may not be possible for us to reliably sell all 1,000 of our fans each and every year, but the idea is that it takes fewer people than you think to make the money you want to make, assuming you are able to sell them something on a reliable and consistent-enough basis.

This means that instead of focusing on having massive reach, you can focus on building deeper relationships.

Money is not made from popularity. It is not made solely from the trade of social currency. Money is made when people are willing to trade their social currency and physical currency for what you sell.

I said at the beginning that there are strategies you can use to increase your social currency with the goal of increasing your physical currency as well.

Let's move into that with a story. This story is about how I began using Twitter. It illustrates how you can first gain attention and then build engagement and grow your social currency in concentric circles from there.

All social currency starts with attention because attention is the first step to making anything else happen. You can build engagement, reputation, or any of the other currencies if nobody is paying attention to you in the first place.

When I first started using Twitter, I had what I termed "tweetfright"—that feeling of having just 140 characters and not knowing what to say. I remember that I used to agonize over what to say, and it always felt really risky unleashing my tweet onto the rest of the world. (Which at that time, was actually more like 25 people.) Yet the more comfort I gained with this platform, the more I began to share.

Not everything resonated for my followers, but when it did, they began to retweet what I'd said, and that helped more people come to know of me. So, for my initial followers, I had their attention mostly because I knew them in real life, and we were adding on to our existing connection by also connecting online. So in this first circle, I had attention. When my first circle began commenting and interacting with me, I had engagement. When they began to share my content, they helped me gain attention of a second circle of followers. This second circle began to engage, and shared my content, helping me gain attention to a third circle of followers—and so on.

It takes fewer people than you think to make the money you want to make.

If you think about growing your currency in concentric circles, starting in closest with the people you know best and building it out from there, this process will likely make a lot of sense to you.

It's not much different than growing your circle of friends in real life either. You may have two friends with whom you share six types of social currency—you pay attention to each other, connect with each other, know, like, and trust each other. Then one of these friends brings a new friend into your circle. You meet this new person, willing to give them attention because s/he is a friend of your friend. Then, if you like this new person, you might be willing to engage with him or her more, and the more you engage, the more you can come to know them, like them and trust them. It's the same process that happens both online and offline.

Engagement is the process of turning attention into action. It's when the passive reading of your status update turns into a "like" or a "comment." It's what's happening when someone adds on to something you've said, or contributes a new perspective to the conversation. As a term, engagement is over-used lately, but still represents an important concept. In terms of your profitability, engagement is the first action people take to learn more about you and what you do.

People must take an action to even be in the running to be one of your true fans.

REPUTATION

This is what people say, think, and feel about you when you're not around. It is built by a series of consistent behaviors over time. It takes a lot to build a strong reputation, but it doesn't always take a lot to lose your strong reputation. One unexpected and significant lapse and your reputation can take a serious hit.

Our goal is to build a reputation for consistency and to be known for delivering results.

CHAPTER 10

I wanted to talk about the remaining currencies: being known, liked, trusted, and talked about through the lens of strategies to build true fans.

I have 14 strategies you can use to start building your concentric circles. Let's look at a few of them next.

The first is to determine what it is your clients need. That might sound so basic. I really think it's super important because we all build our businesses a little bit with blinders on. We think that something that we offer is really why people buy from us. In so many cases that I've been part of, either in my own business or where I talk to clients and encourage them to ask the questions, they have found out that what they thought they were selling or why they thought their clients were buying, and why their clients were actually buying were not the same. Whether you're new in business or you've been in business for a while, I would encourage you to find some way to connect with either your three or five best clients, if you have some, or a larger community of people that represent your potential clients. You can do surveys or get some questions answered, and try to really uncover what it is your clients need.

This whole process of building true fans is really about the process of building influence with people, and I mean that in a positive way. Being able to guide them, inform them, educate them, move them to get answers to whatever their problems are. You don't even necessarily need to support people with just your own products or services. Sometimes knowing a lot about many different areas can make you a really good sounding board or can make you a really good resource that people would benefit from knowing about.

It's about positioning yourself as a trusted advisor or trusted resource.

When you look at all the ways that you can serve your clients you want to first be sure that you understand what they need. Do they need support? Do they need advice? Do they need direct

143

help? Do they need you to do work for them in some way to offer them some kind of done-for-you service? What are the skill sets you bring? What are the skill sets that have created the most income for you so far?

I have a quick, funny story about that. When I look back at all of the skill sets I have, the technical skill sets that I have that enable me to build authority websites have actually been probably, singlehandedly, the largest producer of income for me over the past few years. I have a doctorate in psychology. I have a coaching business. I do different kinds of business consulting as well. In terms of the largest income at this time, it has been in this process of turning technical ideas like search engine optimization, blogging, and analytics into easier to understand actionable business wisdom.

It's an interesting thing because if you had asked me what people buy from me, I would have said, "People buy my strategy. They buy my thinking." But when I really look at the numbers in my own business, where my clients have invested the most is in paying for my help to make the technology easier to understand and use for better results. They pay me for the strategy I can create, as well as for the implementation and systems I bring.

If you look back in your business, you might find as I did that you have specific domains where you create the largest sources of revenue. The first strategy is to understand what your clients need.

The second strategy is to listen. That is both when you are asking clients what they need and it's also when you start new relationships with new potential clients or new potential referral sources. The people who are on the front lines of experiencing a problem that you solve are the ones that have the most up-to-date and timely information about what would help them. You can be a business innovator simply by listening to what people are looking for and asking them how they think they'd like to see the problem solved. Very often people who are living with the problem on a daily basis have some insight about what they need to make a change or what would be an ideal solution for them.

Let's look at this through an example. Let's use a day planner. If you plan your schedule in an appointment book or something like that, you may have a specific brand of appointment book that you really like that you've been using forever. One year, though, the manufacturer changes the spacing and you used to have two lines to write your appointments and now you only have one. You look at that appointment book and you say, "I can still use it. That's fine. But I used to write extra notes on the second line and I can't do that anymore." If you were asked about your feelings about that day planner now, you would probably have really good feedback and be able to say, "I've used it for the past 10 years. I really don't like this change because this is how I used that second extra line that you got rid of." A company that maybe is seeing a decrease in planner sales because of the changes, would be really, really wise to listen to you as a customer who has a history with the product and is noticing some things that would make it better going forward. That is kind of a trivial example perhaps because there are lots of other day planners and there are probably other ways you can keep track of your schedule. Even with something as small as that, the person who has front line knowledge, which is you in this case, can offer some ideas of how a product or service can be made better. For all of us, our clients and customers can do the same thing. Strategy two is to listen.

The third strategy is to define your brand. Branding is a huge topic area that I won't attempt to cover here in depth, but you might think of branding as what people say about you when you're not in the room. When you have a defined brand and people know what you stand for, you're automatically going to get a lot more attention. The way that our brains work is they try to always categorize information, making it easy to group together and easy to find. When people don't understand what you do or they have no idea about how you work, they have no category or no bucket to put you in, so you're not very memorable. When they know more specifically what it is you offer, how you work, what you do, maybe they are cued in by the colors you use or the words you use or the way you conduct yourself, you start to build a category in their mind. Ideally, we want it to be a category of one where you're the only person that they know with that. You're the only person that can fill that space in their brain about that category.

The important thing about branding, leaving aside all the graphics and all the things that go with branding, is you really need to know what you stand for and you really need to communicate it. That's what gets people's attention. You have an opinion. You share it. You're not afraid to stand up for what you believe to be really true. You're not afraid to make outcomes that line up with what you believe to be true.

Using an example from my own business, I'm really, really passionate about clients being able to be more profitable. That theme runs through everything I do. It doesn't matter if I'm coaching somebody or I'm working on their search engine optimization. It doesn't really matter the work that I do. I'm always looking at how we can tie this back to their cash flow. I really try to keep the idea in Profitable Popularity as being profitability first and popularity second. If you have a theme you always find yourself working on with clients, that would probably be a good place to begin to define your brand and to make that belief system much more evident.

Another strategy for building true fans is to tell stories. Stories are our oldest form of communication. They're the way that we understand about the world. They're the way that we learn new information. Again, I said before that our brains work by categorizing information. Stories help us do that. Stories that have a beginning, middle and end are the ones that are remembered the best because people expect that flow. They expect that when you start a fairy tale with, "Once upon a time in a far away land," that ultimately it's going to end with something like, "They lived happily ever after."

There is obviously a way to make use of stories that are incomplete. Sometimes you'll watch movies where the ending comes abruptly or there are a lot of questions left unanswered. Those definitely have power, too. I don't think they work as well for marketing purposes, though. Remember how I said people want to make good decisions without working too hard? They're not going to spend a lot of time figuring out the intricacies or the missing points or the gaps. They're going to move on to something else. Where people may take brain power to try to figure out the ending to a movie or figure out a parallel alternate ending, they're not going to probably spend that much time trying to understand your particular business offering or your particular business story.

When you're looking to tell stories about your business, there are two important elements to remember (and you'll see these again in the chapter on creating and using content). The first element is to create a context for the story. When you're giving updates in social media, the ones that get more attention are the ones that give people a little bit of background and context to whatever it is you're updating. People sometimes post really random things on Facebook and they get no engagement because nobody understands what that person is talking about. They don't have a frame or a relevancy for what that person is referring to. Even in small things like Twitter updates or Facebook status updates, see how you can give some contextualization.

The other way that people pay more attention when you tell stories is when you use emotions in your stories. Emotions are processed more deeply in the brain, and emotions impact the way we think, judge, and reason. To the extent that you can give contextual, emotional, and relevant information in your business stories, you'll have more attention. When you have more attention you have more opportunities to turn those people into fans. Your stories should inform, inspire, educate, or entertain. Be sure they have the underpinnings of context, relevancy, and emotions as well.

The next strategy to building true fans is to create as many touch points as you can. To my way of thinking, a touch point a marketing channel by which potential true fans can find you. This idea of creating touch points is one that needs a little bit of explanation, I think. It's probably an area that most of us could focus more on. One of the biggest mistakes I see in the way that people promote themselves online is they don't create enough avenues for new people to find them. They start their blog and they post there when they can. They maybe post their content to Facebook as well. They have a certain community there. They have a certain community on Twitter, or a certain community on LinkedIn, or a certain community on Pinterest, and so on. They actually don't look to create any kind of coordinated conversation or coordinated effort among all of those sites. Or, they only use one site at a time rather than using multiple sites at once. What this refers to is taking the content you create for your main marketing avenues and using technology to spread and share it so it reaches many places at once. I'm still advocating that you focus on three core marketing avenues—that hasn't changed. I'm now also adding in this next element, that of widespread distribution, so your excellent content reaches more people more easily. This is done very well with technology.

While we won't be able to go into the specifics of how to set this up here, the idea is that the more touch points you can create both in terms of channels where more people can find you and how many times you connect with them through those channels on a regular basis, you're creating many more opportunities to turn interested bystanders into true fans. This process is about turning your three core marketing avenues into many channels of distribution so that you can be found and can attract more targeted people into your community.

There's a piece of psychological research that says that familiarity breeds likeability, especially when a person is perceived as providing good information or value. What that means is the more familiar you can make yourself to people through the use of videos, audio, writing on your blog, sending out a newsletter regularly, and so on, the more likable you will become—if your information is good. I'm assuming your information is good.

The simplest way to understand this is that the more you share your information out in the world with people who are interested, the more interest you'll generate. The more interest you generate, the greater the likelihood that those people will move further into conversation and connection with you, which is really the next step of moving into true fandom. Interest creates more interest.

The final strategy I want to share here is one that is very meaningful to me. It's about being in integrity.

When growing your business, really work to deliver on your promises. This is really the issue of building integrity within yourself and within your business relationships. People remember you when you do what you say. I had an interesting experience a couple of days ago where I had reached out to somebody and asked for more information about what they did. The lady I spoke with was really, really nice. She said, "Oh, my gosh. I'm so glad you called. It sounds like we'd be a perfect fit for you. Let me go ahead and send you some information and I'll follow up in a couple of days and we'll see how we can work together." I was like, "Wow, that sounds great." They seemed like they knew what I needed. They seemed like they were very responsive. They seemed like they would be a really great fit. Guess what happened.

Nothing.

I have yet to receive the information I was promised. I have not received any kind of follow up whatsoever. I'm left kind of sitting in this funny place wondering, "Did they not send it to me? Did it not make it to me? Should I take the next action? Should I not? Should I find someone else?" Again, none of us wants to work that hard. We want people to follow through on what they promise, especially when they promise to send us something or do something that makes our decision making easier.

I see this concept of building true fans as central to building your online social presence, and then, eventually, increasing your profitability. The best use of all the social media platforms and all of the large scale marketing approaches is to enable you to build attention and interest on a broad scale. Technology can assist you in making the initial connections much easier.

Yet even if a relationship begins with the aid of technology, ultimately, all relationships are made one person at a time. I've seen it in my own business. I've seen it in my clients' businesses. My clients who focus on providing really good value delivering on their promises generate the kind of word of mouth interest and word of mouth influence that you can't pay for. Their clients talk about them and share them because they're so moved by the care and service and, I guess you could call it love that my clients deliver.

I have clients who have built whole businesses on referrals simply because they did such a good job of caring for the clients that they had and delivering on the promises they made that their clients were compelled to share them with other people. Take a look at the things you're promising and see if there's a way to improve on what you're promising and what you deliver.

There's so much more I could say, but I hope the ideas I shared here will be helpful to you in thinking about how to grow your own social capital and use this in the service of cultivating true fans.

Chapter 11

METRICS & MEASUREMENT IN YOUR BUSINESS

ONE OF THE biggest missing pieces in most businesses is the absence of measurements and data. Too many important business decisions are made based on feelings, without enough facts.

There are three large categories to measure in your business. The first category is what we might call key performance indicators-these are your own areas of priority. At minimum, these should include earnings and expenses and rate of business growth. You have to know the numbers of what you are earning and spending, and whether your business is bringing in enough money to sustain your lifestyle.

After that, the second area to measure, in terms of your online marketing, is how many visitors are coming to your website (traffic). The third area to measure is what actions your website visitors are taking (conversion). We'll focus first on website traffic.

The reason I'm including such a lengthy overview of traffic is because most people have no idea why their online business isn't performing better.

Many times, potential clients approach me about generating more visitors to their websites. They come to our initial conversation feeling perplexed and confused about why they aren't receiving more phone calls from their websites.

They fiddle with the colors. They get a new header graphic. They take new pictures. Some (the more tech savvy of the bunch) add widgets and toolbars and all kinds of flashy add-ons to try to get attention.

Yet it still doesn't work.

In fact, just in the past few weeks of working on this book, I've had four conversations with potential clients who are feeling desperate and anxious about how their websites are not performing. In every single one of these four cases, as well as numerous others over the past few years, when I review their site, I find that they are not measuring their website visitors or traffic. What this means is that they don't know for sure if nobody is seeking their services because nobody is coming to the site (a problem of not enough traffic) OR if nobody is calling because the site is not useful and compelling (a problem of not enough conversion).

These are two different problems which need to be assessed and resolved distinctly. If the problem is one of not enough traffic, then we expect that sending more traffic should create inquiries and/or sales. If the problem is one of conversion, then we will see that even if we send more traffic, it is unlikely to result in more inquiries or sales.

You have to have adequate traffic levels first, before you can tackle the issue of conversion, so this is a two-step process. First, assess the traffic levels, and then assess how this traffic is responding to the site. Once you have information about these two factors, you know better what problem(s) you're trying to solve.

In these cases, the first thing I suggest is the installation of traffic tracking software. This software requires you to place a special code on your website, and it tracks when people visit your site, how long they stay, how many pages they visit, and can also track whether they sign up for your email newsletter or some other free gift. It can track where they come from geographically and if they are visiting your site using a mobile device.

Does this give you some idea of how much information you could have access to? It's a lot and it's very valuable because it's specific data about your business. I've been able to help my clients use this data to drive business decisions about where to market, how much to market, what to sell, and how to build reputation and credibility. It's really powerful.

There are several options you have for traffic tracking software, but the one I like and recommend for most people is the free Google Analytics. (http://Google.com/Analytics)

If you have a Google account, and you most likely do (or can get one, these are free as well), then you can set up an Analytics account and get this installed on your website.

Once the account is set up, Google Analytics will provide you a tracking code to install or have installed on your website. If you use Wordpress for your site, there are several good plugins which make this super easy to do. Once the tracking is successfully installed, Google Analytics will start tracking data for you.

It usually takes about 24 hours for data to appear in your Google Analytics account, and data will be collected automatically as long as the tracking code remains on your site.

When Analytics is properly installed and working correctly, it will give you a wealth of specific information about your business.

Next, I want to spend a bit of time reviewing the Google Analytics data you're collecting and what it actually means.

Whether you are completely new to Google Analytics or have been using it for a while, I believe you will find something valuable in this chapter.

If you're newer to Analytics, we'll be looking at what kinds of data Google Analytics can give you about your website or blog and the traffic that you get to the site. If you're more experienced with Analytics, we'll also discuss how you can link the different numbers in Google Analytics to measurable results in your business.

This means that measurement is not just to view how many site visitors you're getting, though that's important, but also to understand how these numbers can show if your visibility and credibility and influence are growing. I see this data as more than just numbers, but as offering some insights into the health of your business in some key areas.

If you are like many people and want to avoid the numbers, I understand! But please stick with it. Understanding these numbers has the power to transform your business.

The purpose of taking these measurements is to see how you can increase your business profitability. Remember when I said earlier that popularity wasn't enough? I don't want you to get overly caught up in "how many friends do I have?" and "how many people are following me?" without a grasp on profitability.

Measuring some key areas in your business will help you with greater certainty if your marketing is creating positive returns.

Measuring without a business plan has no purpose except as an ego feed. What I mean by that is if you are measuring thousands of things on your website, and you're spending so much time on measuring that you have no chance to understand or synthesize what the data is telling you, you're sort of measuring without purpose.

But on the other hand, if you're not measuring at all it means you're probably leaving money on the table and getting less return on your business investment.

So the idea is to find the right metrics to measure and to measure those regularly and to make time to understand what the data means and is showing you about your business.

When I think about building influence and recognition online, I think of it as a three-part cycle, consisting of visibility, credibility and influence.

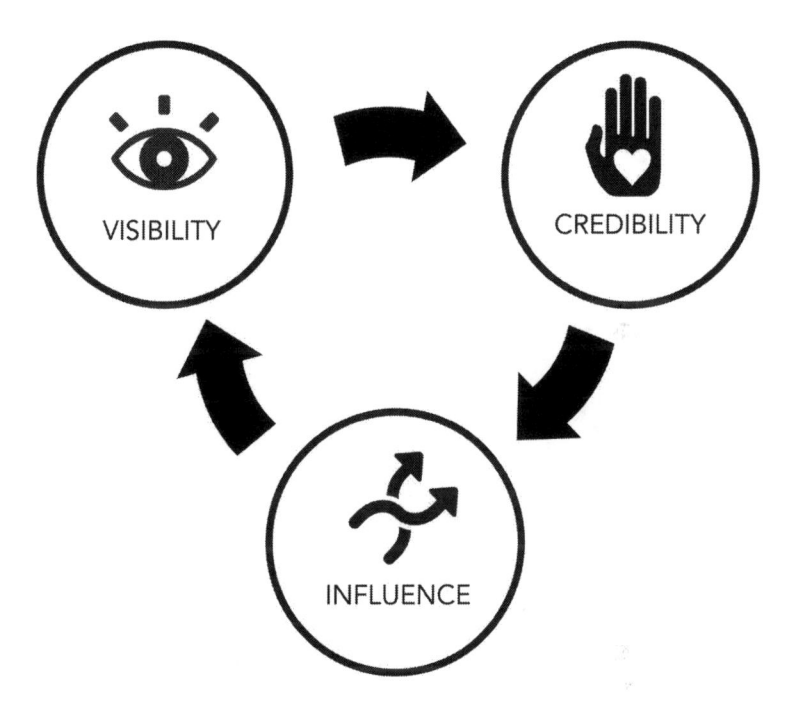

FIGURE 11:1: The circle of visibility, credibility and influence

As we go through the Google Analytics measures that we're going to be talking about next, you'll see that we'll be talking about different measurements and they all relate to this idea of building influence, building visibility or building credibility. When you're looking at promoting yourself online, when you have really high levels of influence, high levels of credibility and high levels of visibility, you can actually get away with a lot more self promotion than people who don't have those items. If you are focused right now on building your influence, visibility and credibility, you're laying a strong foundation for being able to promote your services and products later.

INTERNET MARKETING FOR THE REST OF US

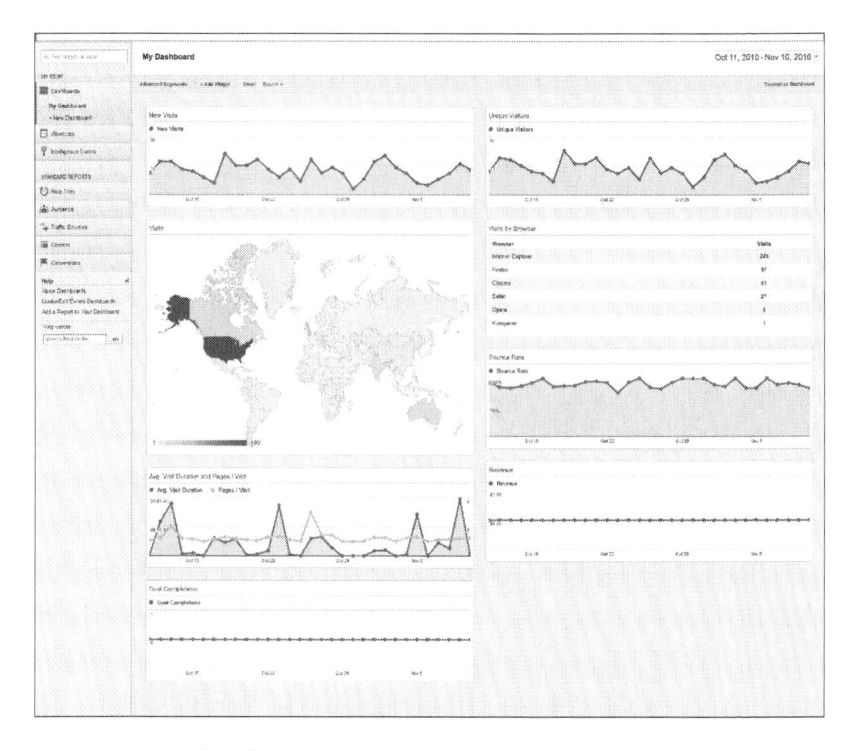

FIGURE 11-2: Google analytics screenshot

This analytics screenshot represents what you will see after your Google Analytics has been capturing data for a while. You can log in, and you're given what's called the "dashboard view." It looks exactly like this. The peaks and valleys in the graph are probably going to look different based on your site's traffic. What you'll see at the top is the dashboard overview and all the different statistics and all the different pages that you're going to go through.

What you're really looking for on this first page is just to get a sense of how your blog or website is doing. If you look at the two left graph, you'll see that one is defining the highest peak of traffic. You can't really tell right here but it will give you a date or day when you had the highest traffic. You're also just getting a sense of when you had the lowest traffic. It will give you a date or a day that that happened. What you want to see is a generally even set of data where your blog is getting at least the same amount of traffic regularly.

You will have days where your traffic declines, such as around holidays or in the summer, but you just want to make sure the declines are not too extreme.

In this screenshot, what you're seeing with this blog is that there was a time when this blog wasn't regularly updated. That accounts for the valley just before the first arrow.

When the site updated, the traffic rose again, but then when it wasn't updated for a while, the traffic dropped again. If you have a blog but are not blogging regularly, your traffic will likely look something like this.

What you need to understand about this graph, overall, is that this graph shows how your traffic is growing. The higher the peaks, the better, and the more of them, the better.

You can see that at a glance. You can also adjust this view by a date range in the upper right hand corner so you can look back three months, you can look back just one day. You can adjust it within Google Analytics itself. You want to see how your traffic flow is, and more traffic is better, typically speaking.

I say typically speaking because if we look at the second panel, the map in the center of the page, this tells you where the percentage of your traffic is coming from around the world. The darker the color, the more traffic you are receiving from that geographical location

If you are a US-based blogger and you're selling products and services in the US, you definitely want the United States to be darker in this view because it means that you're getting a majority of US traffic. They're going to be in a position to buy what you're selling. It's not uncommon that you will also get readers from around the world, but you would want and expect that these will be fewer than your more desirable US-based traffic.

INTERNET MARKETING FOR THE REST OF US

If you have an international product or you can serve clients internationally you want to definitely have the US but you probably want to also have color across the whole world. I work with a lot with clients from the UK and Australia. On some of my sites I can tell that I'm getting a good amount of people coming from those countries. You just want to take a look and make sure that your map overlay is attracting the people that you are geographically interested in reaching.

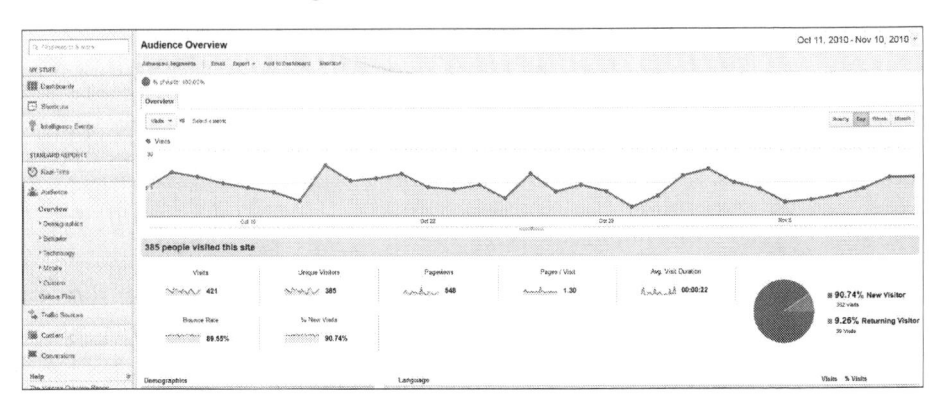

FIGURE 11-3: Visitor dashboard screenshot

This next screen is the Visitor's Overview Panel. At the top you have a graph that talks about what your visitor profile is, how many people have come on a particular day. If you find a peak on a particular day that's significantly higher than any of the other days, you definitely want to look at what kind of content you wrote on that day. Most of the time the peaks will match up to a blog post that you published, or a blog post that you published that just got syndicated, or it was shared widely, or somehow just received a lot of attention. You want to watch for this. If you have a spike in traffic, understand what you did to generate that spike.

If you're looking at the screen there are going to be a few numbers that you want to pay attention to specifically. The top tells you the number of visits. In this time period from October 11th to November 10th the site got 421 visits. That's in that whole month. It's not a very highly trafficked site. The number of visits will give you a sense of how many people are coming to your site. The number just under it will tell you how many of them are absolutely unique. What that means is this blog is getting 385 absolutely unique people. A small percentage of those are returning. That's how we get the 421. You want to look at the number of visits and higher is better. You also want to see that number increasing over time because it means that your marketing is working.

If we look at the right most column, the one that says "Avg Visit Duration" that tells you the average time on site. That tells you how long people are staying on your site. This number is really low. What you really want is for people to stay for at least a minute or more. You definitely will get that if you write good content or you have videos of a few minutes in length. What you're seeing here in this blog is that people are coming to this site and because it hadn't been updated lately they're just leaving right away. So in 20 seconds they're coming, they're seeing that nothing has happened and they're leaving. The time on site is really, really low.

I look at time on site as a measure of engagement. My goal is to keep people on my site as long as possible because that's how I know they're engaged with my content. You also want your page views to be high. We didn't talk about that much but that's the third number from the top. The page views number refers to how many pages deep people go into your site. The average page views tells you pages per visitor. This blog is getting about 1.3 page views per visitor. That means they're going to 1.3 pages on average. They're basically coming to a page and leaving. That's not engaging them. As this blog got updated regularly what you'd expect to see is that the number of page views goes up, the number of visitors should go up, the time on site should go up as well.

Sites that have a high time on site tend to be seen as more authoritative in Google and they tend to get better rankings in the search engines. That leads us to our next measurement which is the fourth arrow. That's bounce rate.

Bounce rate is actually a measure of how quickly visitors leave your site. Bounces happen when people search on something and come to your site, but they leave quickly just after. It can actually be a way of understanding how well your marketing is pulling the people that you want to track.

Let's say for example—and we've all had this experience—we go to a search engine. We look up dog training. We find a result that is interesting to us. We click on it and the site has nothing to do with dog training. They just optimized for that word maybe accidentally or intentionally. Anyway, they've optimized for the word so they're getting clicks. But because the content is not what you expect, you quickly leave. This act of visiting and quickly leaving soon after will increase the site's bounce rate. You can think of the bounce rate like a bouncing ball. People come in and they bounce or they leave right away. That also is a measure of quality. It's a subtle factor but you really want your bounce rate to be as low as possible. Something about 50% or less is good, and even lower than that is even better. A low bounce rate means that your website is really attracting people who are engaged in your content and are interested, and they're spending some time there.

Finally, if we look at the bottom value in the second column, that tells you percentage of new visits. There's a little bit of debate that I have about new visits. Obviously, if you're looking at building your reach you want to have a high percentage of new visits. That means that new people are hearing about you and they're coming. A high percentage of new visits with a lot of page views and a lot of time on site basically means that your marketing is working because you're attracting people and they're hanging out on your site. You also want to have a balance between new visits and returning visitors. It does me no good if you come to my site just once for two minutes and you don't sign up for my list or you don't take any other action and I have no way to reach you again. I would suggest that for new visits you want to try to get to about 50% new visits and 50% returning visits.

The other thing I want to point out is if your site is fairly new, the bulk of your visits are going to be new visits. Over time, perhaps within a six month period, it is desirable to see the percent of new visits reach some kind of equilibrium with the number of returning visitors.

The people who return to your site two or more times are the people who are interested enough to give you more of their attention. These are the people who will have had multiple connections or multiple contacts with you. They're going to be the ones that move further into the buying process, the buying funnel. If you have too low a number of new visits it means that your site isn't really growing. You aren't reaching enough new people. Depending on your business model, depending on what you sell and how you sell it, it may be fine. You may just have a totally pure returning-customers-only type business. That's wonderful and great if it works for you and works for your business. However, at some point, you will need to reach new people as you will, one day, have sold everything you can to everyone who already knows of you. So try to find a balance between retaining visitors and attracting new ones. I mentioned about reaching an equilibrium between the two. My general suggestion is to try to create some kind of dynamic balance: 60/40; 50/50, between returning visitors and new visitors. You want to find a way to engage with the returning visitors and bring new people into your sphere as well.

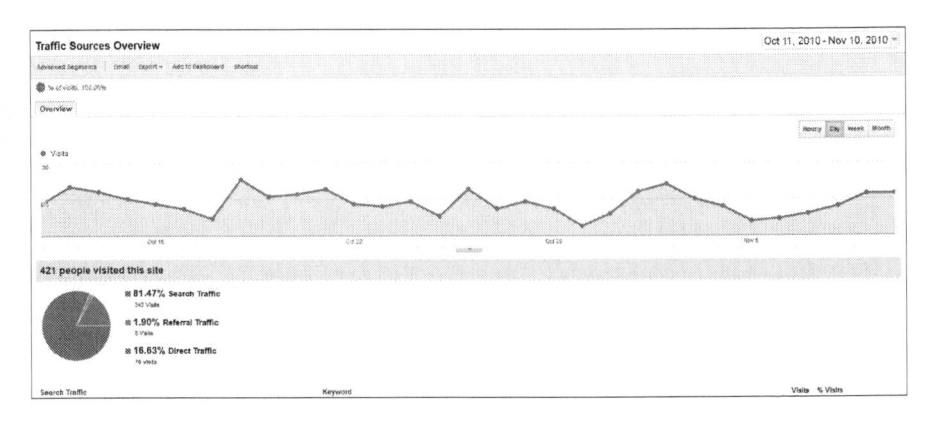

FIGURE 11-4: Traffic sources screenshot

In this next panel, we're looking at traffic sources. There are a couple of things you want to pay attention to here. The middle panel has a pie chart which tells you how your traffic is divided up. It tells you that out of 421 visits, 16.63% came directly which means they typed the URL of the site in their browser. That means that basically it's a measure of how many people have heard of this site and are coming to this site by choice. It can also sometimes be people clicking a link from somewhere else and coming to your site that way. Sometimes sites which are sending traffic don't show up as referrers, as you would expect, and so they show up in the direct traffic numbers. Returning back to the screenshot, you'll also see that a small percentage, approximately 1.9%, is "referring sites" which means other sites linking to this. 81.4% is from search engines which means the site is ranking in the search engines and receiving visitors from that placement.

What you can see here is that the bulk of traffic is coming from the search engines and then followed by people hearing about the site URL. There wasn't a lot of linking done on this site so there aren't many referring sites. The thing to look at here is direct traffic, which means that people have heard of you.

You would expect that number to go up if you're doing a lot of self promotion, especially face to face. If you're doing a lot of speaking where you're meeting people, networking, things like that on a large scale, you would expect your direct traffic to go up because they would be looking at your business card and typing in your URL. If you're doing a lot of search engine optimization, you're doing a lot of social media optimization, you'd expect referring sites and search engine sites to be high.

The top value in the pie chart tells you what percentage of traffic is coming from your search engine sources. Google is typically going to be the highest for almost everybody because Google drives the most Internet traffic. I've not seen too many situations where any other search engine was sending more traffic than Google, if the site was receiving search engine traffic at all.

The Content panel can also give you some understanding of what your visitors are viewing on your site and what they are searching for when they come to your site.

This gives you a list of keywords that people search for and click through to your site. You can drill down into this section and get a more complete report of the top keywords. What you want to do periodically, like every couple of weeks or even a little more often if you're stuck for content ideas, is log in to your Google Analytics, come to the sources overview panel and start looking at the keywords people are using to come to your site.

There was a particular blog that I ran where, in one month's time, I was receiving 30-40% of my visitors based on one blog post. It was about how to fire a client. (I think for whatever reason people were having a lot of client issues in that month!) Now, logging in and seeing that, I had some choices that I could make as a business owner. I could have written more content about that issue. I could have written an ebook. I could have offered a teleseminar. I could have done some other business promotion or marketing promotion based on the fact that I was getting so much traffic to that one blog post. There are more ways to use it. That's just one example of how you can use the keywords to drive your content and to see what it is people want from you.

In doing this review, the other element to look for is whether you are receiving visitors on random keywords you're not expecting. If this is the case, your site content needs to be tweaked because you are likely ranking for searches you don't want to rank for, and that you might not be able to benefit from. In the full list of keywords, there will be some throwaway/random keywords you rank for. That's OK, as long as it's just a few. Except for these few, you want all of your keywords to be related to the main point of your site or blog otherwise you're writing content that's not targeted enough.

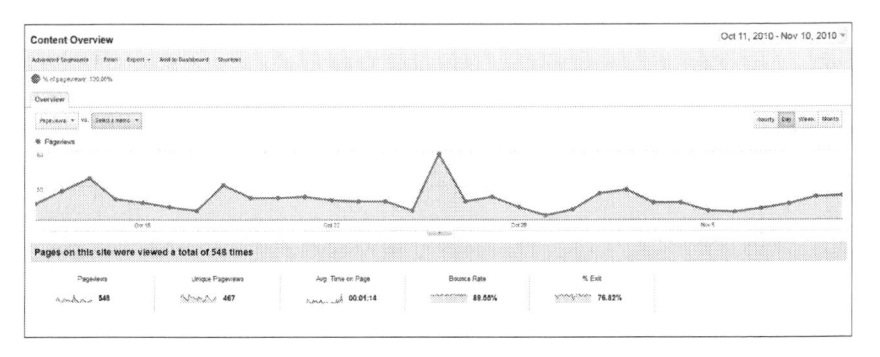

FIGURE 11-5: Content overview panel screenshot

The last panel we're going to go through is the content overview panel. At the top we have an arrow and that tells you how many page views. It tells you how many pages people have looked at on the site. How many of them were unique views. So 467 at the second arrow is the number of unique views. Then it tells you the bounce rate again and we talked about that. The bounce rate is high on this blog.

Also on this page, in your Analytics account, you'll see on the right hand side a listing of pages. These reflect which content on your site is most popular. You can use this data to help you decide what to focus on more deeply. The idea is that if you find that some of your content is getting really high page views, you want to see if there's a way that you can benefit from that in terms of your profitability or in terms of seizing an opportunity into that opening.

There is much more data that Analytics provides, but these measures are a strong place to begin from. For the more advanced business owner, Analytics enables you to set up testing so you can see which pages are working best. You can also see exactly how visitors move through your site, so you can see if your sales funnel is working as planned. These are just two examples of how you can use Analytics and this kind of tracking to create a living snapshot of your business.

I was recently speaking with one of my clients, Lissa Boles (http://www.thesoulmap.com) and walking her through an analysis of her site traffic on a recent campaign (http://30days30dares.com). From reviewing her site statistics, I could identify for her places where she might be able to make some changes in order to create more sales. We talked about how traffic was flowing, which places on her site were receiving the most interest and attention, and how she might make more compelling offers there, so that her offers could be seen by more people. We looked at which pieces of her site were drawing the most attention, and where she might want to emphasize or highlight more.

Lissa explains, *"This type of data is absolutely invaluable to have about my business. I can make decisions based on what is actually happening, not what I think is happening. I can't imagine anyone running their business without this level of information."*

This is just one of many wonderful examples of how to use this kind of business data to make business decisions.

People sometimes go vague or feel confused or stupid or uncomfortable about this numerical kind of business data.

Don't worry if this sounds like you! Most of us start out that way. But the good news is that this can be learned: just start slowly and stick with it. Seek to understand just one statistic today. Feel comfortable with it. Add another in tomorrow. Feel comfortable with it. Add a third in after that. And so on. Little by little, you will come to understand this.

After key indicators and website traffic, the third set of measurements you want to chart for your business is the rate of conversion you have. Conversion means how many people take an action based on your marketing. Higher conversion means more people take action, lower conversion means fewer people take action.

How can you know if your next program is going to fill? Without conversion numbers, you really can't. But imagine this:

What if you knew that for every 15 people you invited to your program, three would sign up? Then, if you wanted six people in your program, you would know that you'd have to invite about 30 people. That's conversion in action.

Conversion means you track what you did to generate an action. Then you convert this to a percentage.

So if you reach 100 people with your newsletter, and one signs up for your program, that is a 1% conversion rate (one person in every hundred will sign up).

If you invite 15 people and 3 sign up, that is a 20% conversion rate. (3 divided by 15 multiplied by 100).

Tracking your conversion rate gives you an idea of how much marketing and promotion you need to do in order to generate the profitability you want.

This came up recently in a coaching call with one of my clients, Janet Slack (http://www.solopreneur.biz). Janet has been considering some shifts in her business model, moving from working with larger groups to working with smaller ones. She finds small group and individual work very satisfying and would like to do more of it.

When she raised this desire, we began discussing a few different approaches she could take to begin this shift. She decided to begin by offering intensive one day paid workshops on different topics, and then, from there, inviting people to consider individual coaching with her.

Her results are very fresh as I write this. In her first run of this model, she had 15 people sign up for her intensive one day workshop, and from there, six people expressed interest in perhaps working with her individually, and subsequently completed an application for a discovery/strategy session, AKA individual consultation.

From the group of 15 who attended the intensive, six people wanted to continue the conversation. Janet's conversion rate from workshop to discovery session is 6/15 * 100= 40%. This means that, roughly, every time she has 10 people in her one day workshop, she can be certain that about four will want to discuss individual coaching. (Yes, the data is very new, so we have to see if this holds up in the next offering. But assuming it does, Janet will have good business data to move forward with.)

So, then, she has 40% conversion to her discovery sessions. From these six discovery sessions, she has had four people sign up to work with her individually. So her conversion rate from discovery session to individual coaching is 4/6 * 100= 67%.

What this tells us is that when Janet can speak with someone individually, two out of three times, they will become her client.

Can you see how valuable this data is?

This means that if Janet wants to get four coaching clients, she knows that she is likely to be able to do this by having a one day workshop with at least 15 people. This becomes a measurement she can lean into and rely on as she plans her business growth.

Understanding conversion in your business enables you to right-size your marketing efforts to match your desired outcomes. You can reduce the waste and strain of "over-marketing" or, as my friend and colleague Andrea J. Lee says, "Using a power tool to drive in a tack."

Conversion rates assist you in putting numerical figures to your business and in being better equipped to make data-driven business decisions about what to pursue next in order to meet your business cash flow and business satisfaction goals.

Keeping track of numbers and data in this way can make your business easier to run, and you can make decisions with greater certainty.

When people sometimes feel avoidant or vague about numbers in their business, I believe this is because they have not deeply understood how those numbers are relevant or what they mean, practically speaking. They have not understood how the numbers provide a living snapshot of the health and growth of their individual business.

While I love metrics and measurement, I don't care about numbers just for numbers' sake. I care because they mean something about my business—they enable me to see patterns and gauge performance. They help me know where to spend more time and where to spend less.

They tell me if my business is reaching people I want to serve and if my influence is rising. They enable me to put facts to my feelings, and find alignment between what I do and the results I see.

In a way, measuring key performance indicators, traffic, and conversion are three ways of tapping into the heartbeat of your business—helping you see, with data, where you are focusing and where you could be focusing. You'll be able to get more return from your business, with less effort, riding the wave of data, rather than drowning in the whirlpool of feelings.

Chapter 12

THE PROFITABLE POPULARITY METHOD

THE GRAPHIC ON page 170 demonstrates my Profitable Popularity Method. It's a three-part system that relies on content, traffic and monetization.

In the upcoming chapters, we'll talk about each of these. Content is information. It can be information you create, information you consolidate, or information you curate. It includes items such as your blog content, newsletters, articles you write, press releases, guest blogs you author, audios and videos you create, and can even include your social media status updates. Content is any kind of information you share that is meant to educate, inspire, entertain, engage, or inform.

The traffic part of this cycle is visitors—real people—who come across your content online (whether it be through an Internet search, on a social media site, or on a content aggregating site such as YouTube or Pinterest). If you went through the "Tree and the Sorceress" chapter, traffic is the river of people who are

FIGURE 12-1:
Circle of content, traffic and monetization

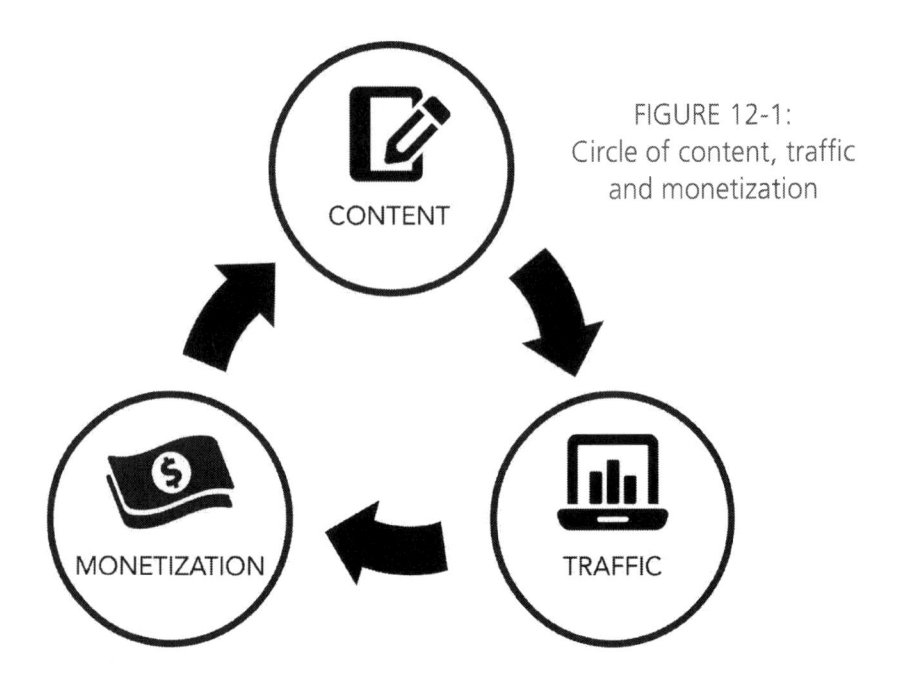

seeking solutions to the problems you solve. Your content drives traffic.

The third part of the cycle, monetization, is the stage where you move these visitors from being interested bystanders to someone who takes the next step and steps up, saying, "Yes. Here's my money. I want to work with you."

This three-part system is the simplest foundational system by which all online businesses run.

If you have no worthwhile content, it is difficult to attract attention and notice. If you have great content, but not enough traffic, you aren't having enough reach, and therefore aren't having many sales conversations. If you have good content and good traffic, but you never move these visitors to buy—even when they have expressed interest in doing so—the monetization portion of this cycle will be weak.

Each time you create content, you have the possibility to generate traffic from it or because of it. Each time you generate traffic, you have an opportunity to monetize. Each time you monetize (such as in offering a workshop, coaching program, or training), you create more content. You can repurpose this content to generate more traffic. This traffic can generate more money. And so on.

In my experience, relevant, meaningful and useful content, combined with content distribution strategies, leads to profitability.

Now let's look in more detail at each segment of this interconnected cycle.

NOTES

Chapter 13

CREATING AND USING CONTENT

AS I'VE ALREADY mentioned, content is information. It can be information you create, information you consolidate, or information you curate.

Content functions as both a conduit and a vehicle for gaining attention and building relationships. Good content can open up the conversation between you and a potential client; in this case, it's acting as a conduit. Good content that is distributed out to the larger Internet can bring you website visitors and newsletter subscribers; in this case, content is functioning as a vehicle.

In both cases, content serves to help you build your business and to reach your business objectives. In a way, you can view content as a 24/7/365 spokesperson for your business.

Good content can serve four worthy domains of your business. It can be used for education. It can be used for marketing. It can be used to build your expert status. It can be used for revenue generation. And of course, it can be used for all of the above. (That's the best kind of good content!)

I remember my first experience with the power of good content. I think it was sometime in 1999 or 2000, when I was gaining in my online marketing skills. One tactic I used quite successfully then was article marketing.

> **Content functions as both a conduit and a vehicle for gaining attention and building relationships.**

As it sounds, article marketing is the process of creating articles and distributing them out to the Internet. The goal of these articles was threefold. First, it was to increase your reach, by exposing your ideas to more people. Second, the objective was to be compelling enough that the reader would want to click through and learn more. Typically, you would try to direct them to an opt-in page so that you could encourage them to join your email list. Third, each time an article was accepted and published, it provided you a link back to your site, which would increase your site's authority (we touch more on backlinks in the chapter on traffic). In any case, I was sending out probably two articles a month in this way.

At that time, the Internet was much less crowded, and people were not as overwhelmed with content, so article marketing worked well. It still does work as a business promotion strategy, though it has experienced some dilution compared to before.

The power of content was driven home to me the day that I received an email from someone I'd never met. She wrote me after coming to my website through one of the articles I'd written and distributed online. The article was "10 Tips for Dealing with Negative Emotions at Work" and this is what she said to me:

"Rachna. I just want to thank you for writing this article. I live in Tanzania, and I came across your article by chance today.

It really helped me because I am going through some difficult circumstances at my job, and I am feeling angry and frustrated all the time. Your article gave me some ideas of how I can handle this differently. Thank you."

OK, now, first, how freaking cool, right? I remember being stunned when I received this email. I was stunned that I could reach out and help someone I'd never met—and more to the point—someone I was unlikely to ever meet. I was thrilled to know that my content was reaching out across the world, and I was, in a sense, making the world better by sharing my ideas. I've never forgotten how I suddenly understood that good content could make a difference.

Not only did I have a platform to share my ideas and refine them, I was able to help people at a distance and to offer support and help in a way that was meaningful to them. This was so much greater than I had imagined.

I share that story because I want to convey how deep my respect is for our capacity to communicate meaningful experiences through our content. With the lowering of the barrier to creating content, as I mentioned earlier, we've seen a rise in low quality content. It's almost as if people can't be bothered to put their words together in a proper way, such that their meaning can be conveyed.

I also think that most entrepreneurs don't see their content as being both a conduit and a vehicle for business growth. They write for their blog because they think they should—not because they are tuned in to sharing something that their audience needs to know. I know I'm over-generalizing here, but I just see that there is a fundamental disconnect in how people view their content creation. They don't see that the time they spend to write their blog post and to do it regularly (good content demands consistency) could open doorways they never imagined.

They see content creation as a chore. Yes, of course it is, especially when the ideas seem slow in coming and the words

> **Content is the foundation upon which your business rests.**

don't flow. But essentially, content is the foundation upon which your business rests. If you can't take time to regularly create good content that reliably serves your people, you will find it very difficult to carve out your category of one.

Does this mean that you have to spend hours creating content each and every day? No. Does it mean you have to have the latest technology and super fancy gadgets and be all high tech? No. (Unless you want to be!)

What it does mean is that you have to have courage and consistency. You have to have courage to find your voice and to share your opinions. You have to have consistency in sharing your ideas so they eventually enter people's awareness and filter through their consciousness. You can't know how much impact you're having with 100% certainty, but I assure you, if you are producing good content regularly—and people are accessing it, you are having meaningful impact.

I've had the experience numerous times where it felt like I was writing just for myself. I'd write a blog post and nobody would comment. I'd share it in social media and it was like I'd gone invisible.

It happens to all of us. But those experiences don't mean we should stop. In fact, did you know that most of the people on the Internet are Spectators? They are unlikely to comment or criticize, but they do observe and read.

This finding came out of work done by Forrester Research, in a system that defined the technographics of the Internet. Technographics means how people are using the Internet. You can research the Techonographic profile of your own target market if you want, using Forrester's free online tool.[3]

If you visit the tool and enter age range 35-44 and do not specify gender, here is what you will see:

23% are Creators, meaning they create content or use the Internet to create and share ideas.

34% are Critics, meaning they may not create content themselves, but they do leave comments and share opinions.

20% are Collectors, which means they aggregate information and share it.

54% are Joiners, meaning they join online communities and likely spend time in social networking.

73% are Spectators, meaning they read and observe, but don't interact and are unlikely to share. This is a huge percentage of the online population and might explain why your blog comments are less than you hoped for.

17% are Inactives, meaning they don't use the internet much or use it for extremely limited and specific purposes, such as reading the newspaper or checking stocks. These tend to be people who get onto the Internet for one specific reason and go offline as soon as that specific reason has been addressed.

This is important information to know if you want to set up metrics to measure the success of your marketing. If your target market is made up of a huge percentage of Spectators,

---

[3] http://empowered.forrester.com/tool_consumer.html

for instance, you may not want to measure campaign success by amount of feedback and dialogue. Instead, you might want to measure it in terms of overall visits, time spent on page, or email subscriptions.

If you are looking to create a campaign to get more people involved, you will likely have more activity by appealing to the Critics than you will to the Creators. Of course, there are exceptions, but the overall framework can help guide your thinking.

After all, if you are looking for results, you want to make sure you're looking in the right place.

So when you look at your own content creation cycle, what do you see? If you truly want to stand out in your market and to generate clients and new business much more easily, you must find ways to systematize and routinize your content creation and promotion. Your content is a way of claiming and developing your thought leadership and business leadership. It's that important.

Strong content enables you to be "everywhere at once." It relies on good, usable information, combined with a solid distribution strategy.

Regularly creating and distributing content is one of the best ways I know to build your expert status, visibility and credibility. My content marketing has routinely attracted new opportunities and greater visibility for me.

For instance: I've been invited to speak to large groups based on an article I wrote. Someone read my article, got in touch with me, and asked me to present. This led to additional follow-up business in the form of three new clients.

I've been asked to write for high traffic websites based on content I've written. By having my articles on these high traffic websites, I've received major media interviews, with publications such as *USA Today,* radio stations such as NPR, and I even became a Contributing Editor for *Seventeen Magazine,* and as part of my work with them, I was a guest on NBC's *Today Show*.

The key piece to note here is that I did <u>nothing</u> extra to pursue these opportunities. I developed my content and promoted it, and these people approached me. None of these opportunities could have happened without my regular habit of content creation and promotion.

I'd like to share with you what works for me. If you don't have a content strategy in place yet, perhaps this will show you that it's not that difficult, and you might decide you want one. If you have a content strategy in place already, maybe you'll gain some ideas of how to round yours out even more.

My content strategy publishes in two main frameworks. First is my blog, where I try to write at least twice per month. I used to have more time to post more often, but I try to generate at least two lengthy blog posts per month. My average blog post is about 800 words. When I had more time, I blogged more, but for now, I can easily do once a month, so I stick with that. I post more often when I can.

My second content strategy is in my twice monthly newsletter. I write an original article for that every two weeks, and my topics center around business growth, business coaching, and marketing. I tend to share my new, original content with my email subscribers first. I focus on building relationships, sharing advice, strategies, good information—not just using my email newsletter for promotions only.

From these two frameworks, I create everything else using the process of repurposing.

In case you are not familiar with the term, repurposing is the process of taking content created for one use, and using some or all of it again for other uses. Repurposing is where your content gets leverage.

Here's what I mean: if it takes you one hour to create a blog post, and you never use it again, you have spent one hour to create one blog post. Now by itself, unless you have a highly trafficked blog to begin with, one blog post alone isn't going to do much for your business. This is where I think most people get frustrated. They spend hours of time creating content but see no appreciable improvements in their business.

To my way of thinking, this is because they have not leveraged their content enough; they have not repurposed their content enough to get results. What if, just for example, you took that one blog post you wrote and used that same content in 10 other ways? (And that, in fact, is what I recommend—that you look at how each piece of content can be used in at least 10 ways.)

The 10 ways could be to create more content, to create more traffic, or to create more monetization. Let me show you what I mean, using one of my hallmark examples of 21 ways to repurpose a blog post.

The process of repurposing is essentially creating one piece of content and then adding or subtracting other content to suit your business purpose.

Here's a snapshot of repurposing opportunities I see:

You write your blog post and put it on your blog. *That's use #1.*
▼
Then you take your blog post and convert it to an article for distribution. *That's use #2.*
▼
Then you take a grouping of your articles and make a paid or free document (ebook or short report). *Use #3.*
▼
Then you record your article into an audio and generate a podcast. *Use #4.*
▼
Then you create a slideshow from your article content. *Use #5.*
▼

Then you combine the slideshow and audio together and create a video. *Use #6.*

▼

Then you take your article content and turn it into a teleclass. Use #7. And/or a webinar. *Use #8.*

▼

Then you take the concept or idea from the article and write a press release about it. *Use #9.*

▼

You can group your audios together to create a full length training CD. *Use #10.*

▼

You can bundle each element in some way to make a free or paid product. *Use #11.*

▼

You can use your article as the basis to pitch a reporter on a story. *Use #12.*

▼

You can use it to create a tips booklet. *Use #13.*

▼

You can use it to create a workbook. *Use #14.*

▼

You can use it as content for your ezine. *Use #15.*

▼

You can use it as the basis for a new speaking topic. *Use #16.*

▼

You can use it to create pages for a published book. Use #17.

▼

You can use it in your membership site. *Use #18.*

▼

You can post it as content on Facebook,
Twitter, or LinkedIn. *Use #19.*

▼

You can use it to create a coaching program. *Use #20.*

▼

You can share it as a full length article
on the document sharing sites. *Use #21.*

And I could keep going, but I think you get the idea.

Do you see how powerful this can be?

Yes, of course, converting it to these different formats does require more work, but—and this is important—you are creating more value, too.

Not only are you giving your ideas a lot of room and care and attention—oxygen and room to grow—you are also meeting the needs of your audience, who might like to consume content in various formats.

You are creating more business assets from your original idea. This is giving you more leverage and more use out of the time you took to develop the idea in the first place.

Repurposing is the process of turning your content into other formats so you can create more value, and get more use out of each item you create.

Repurposing is the secret lever—the leverage—that can help you create prolifically, even if you hate to write or it takes a long time for you to express your ideas.

Not all pieces of content are worth sending through this full scale repurposing effort. But for your core ideas—the ideas that you really want to be known for—this type of repurposing offers many benefits.

You save time because you are taking core building blocks and moving them around, rather than starting from scratch. There is a continuity in your expression because all content formats are starting from the same seed. You can get better and more ranking because each type of content format can rank separately.

You can attract new audiences and new markets by having your content available on the various types of distribution platforms.

The extra effort of repurposing is well worth it for the benefits it brings.

Repurposing does require that you develop a certain kind of flexibility in your thinking. Look at how much content you likely have stored on your hard drive that you're not using fully. How could you get it off your hard drive and out into the world, doing good for your business?

Maybe you could quickly generate some free reports and give them away in social media to build your email list? Maybe you could gather your blog posts together and make a Kindle single? Maybe you could record some of your articles into a full length training that you sell?

Or as I have done, maybe you could take bits and pieces from blog posts, speaking presentations, transcripts, newsletters, and begin to knit them together into a full-length book.

There are a lot of possibilities if you open your mind and think about them. In fact, I often have so many ideas for how to use and re-use content that I have to guard against the other problem, that of my ideas starting to become so familiar they feel stale. Although most content does become better with more focus and more polish, it is still important to know how much to work with your content and when it's time to create something new.

For me, I like to balance new ideas with digging more deeply into older ones. I find that most of my clients experience similar kinds of challenges in similar kinds of areas, and I like having already created content I can use to assist them when needed.

With a little creativity, repurposing can enable you to create a consistency in your content, which you can use for greater visibility, credibility, and ultimately, profitability in your business.

"OK," you might be saying, "That's great if I have content I have already created. What about if I'm stumped for new content ideas in the first place?"

I'm glad you asked. I have some ideas for you, too.

One of the best places to get content ideas is by listening to your target audience and the kinds of questions they are asking. You, like me, probably receive email inquiries from people, or maybe you are asked questions when you present on teleseminars or webinars. You see the same kinds of questions popping up again and again. These common questions are a wonderful place to begin when you want to generate content ideas.

Start keeping track of the kinds of questions you're asked over and over, and see if you can create content that addresses these questions. At minimum, you can add this to your website to prequalify your client inquiries. At most, you might be able to convert it into a healthy income stream for your business.

For example, one of my areas of expertise is in building authority websites. When I look back over my business, this arena has been one of my most profitable groups of offerings—the ones centered around using your website better to build your business. If I wasn't that interested in this topic, I could hear the questions from my target market and simply write an article or put up a "frequently asked questions" page and perhaps outsource this work. In my case, though, this happens to be something I like to do, so I've been able to take the common question of "How do I become more well-known online?" and package this into a series of paid programs and services. I've been able to create a healthy and growing income stream from addressing this common question.

Identifying the questions you're asked over and over is one of the best places to begin when searching for content ideas.

Another place to source content ideas is in your own experience. What have you learned now that you wished you knew then? What are all the bits of knowledge that you know that someone else might really want to know?

A third place to generate content ideas is through lots of conversation. Make it a habit to meet new people, read new kinds of books, be exposed to different kinds of ideas. The more new ideas you are exposed to, the more insightful and creative connections you can make.

Two more technical ways to generate content ideas are Google Suggest and industry specific online sites.

You may have noticed that when you go to Google and type in a search query, it gives you a list of "suggestions"—possible search queries you might be looking for or might be interested in. If you're ever stuck for content ideas, try going to Google and typing in some seed keyword phrases. Look at what comes up, and see if the suggestions spark any ideas for you.

A second way to get content ideas is by visiting industry specific online forums or online question sites to see what kinds of questions people are asking. If you're looking for a forum, you can go to Google and type in a phrase like "forum [industry]." This would be something like "forum small business" or "forum automotive care" or "forum knitting." You'll be able to retrieve a list of forums on your specified topic. If you visit the forums and read through some of the threads, you can find topics that people want to know more about. This can give you content ideas, and once the content is created, you might also go back to the forum and share your content appropriately there. Online questions sites are developed around people asking questions and seeking answers. If you want to know what people want to know more about, try visiting sites like Quora.com, where you can ask questions or answer them. Answering questions for other people is a subtle, yet effective way to demonstrate your expertise and might lead to new professional contacts or potential work.

No matter which avenues you choose to generate ideas, once you start having more ideas, it's crucial that you find a way to capture them so they aren't lost. Keep a notepad handy to write them down, or, as I do, keep track of them on a note-taking application on your smartphone.

I generate ideas on a regular basis and create a running list of them, so I always have a place to begin when I want to create new content.

So now we've covered why your business needs content, how to repurpose your content, and how to get ideas for great content.

Before we leave the topic of content, let's discuss a few strategies to make your content more powerful. There are three strategies for this I'd like to share with you here.

The first way to make your content more powerful—that is more memorable and resonant for your audience—is to make sure your content is contextual. This concept of context is even more important when you are sharing updates and information in social media. Social media is a time-shifted medium. This means that people may see your content days after you post it, or perhaps if they don't login to Facebook for a while, they may not see it all. Due to this time-shifted and asynchronous nature of social media, it's more important than ever to create a context for what you're sharing.

The idea of contextualizing your content is one I think about as arising from the research of Piaget, who was a cognitive learning psychologist. Piaget focused on how children learn about the world. His research identified two ways in which children gain information about the world in which they live. The first way is through assimilation and the second way is through accommodation.

Assimilation refers to the idea that we can only learn new ideas that hook onto ideas we already know. So we all carry around what we call a schema or some kind of scaffolding upon which we lay all the new ideas that we get.

The process of assimilation suggests that in order to learn something new, you have to attach it to something you already know. And in that process of attaching it, it then activates accommodation, which is where your schema adjusts to take that in. It's that moment where you perhaps have been stuck in some kind of problem and you can't see any way out of it, and then one day something happens and the door opens, and you can see a solution that you couldn't see before. The moment you see the vexing problem in a new way, accommodation has occurred. It's the process of adjusting what we know to make room for something new.

As I mentioned, Piaget worked mostly with children, but there have been some studies that have been published since looking at adult learning. Hull (1993) found that learning only occurs when you connect information to the learner' frame of reference. What that means for us, practically, is when you are creating and sharing content, it needs to be contextualized for your audience. You need to provide a background. You need to develop a story.

The more that you can help your clients connect the dots in your content, the more attention you will get, the more attention they will pay to it.

The second key to great content is that it needs to be relevant. People tend to remember much more when information is relevant to them and much less when information isn't.

In order for information to be relevant, it must also be timely. If you want to develop expert positioning and stand out as a leader in your field, you must be able to look a bit ahead and speak to what is coming. We know our content is relevant when we can teach people things they don't know or when we can help them understand something that has been puzzling them or troubling them.

We've already discussed the currency of attention, but let me just circle back to it for a moment. In my approach, until you have someone's attention nothing more can happen between you. We want to keep in mind that we need to find ways to get attention.

Current marketing statistics suggest that each of us is exposed to 5,000 or so marketing messages each day. This means we are competing for our client's attention alongside 4,999 other marketers and marketing messages each day.

We want to use all the strategies within our reach to try to be in the front of the client's thinking. Making your content contextual and relevant are two ways to do this.

The third strategy is that content should be emotional. Emotional stories are one of the absolute best ways to get attention and to have people understand your meaning. The reason for that from a neuroscientific perspective is that emotions are processed in a deep part of the brain, the limbic system, which sends connections out to the rest of the brain.

Emotions impact how we view situations and how we feel about them. We can effect changes in people's emotions by the words we write and the stories we share. The more you can generate emotional experiences in the content you create and share, the more attention people will give to your content. If your content generates emotions, your audience will spend more time with it and will give it more attention.

There is more we could talk about in terms of making your content more powerful, but for now, these three pieces are a good place to begin.

Before we move on to the next chapter, I want to cover two more topics: evergreen content and content syndication.

EVERGREEN CONTENT

Evergreen content, as it sounds, is content which is always relevant and useful. It is content based on solid principles of human psychology, behavior, or on scientific laws or repeatable patterns. It is content which will always be "in fashion" and worthwhile.

The contrast to evergreen content might be trendy content or content about "fads." Celebrity content would also count here. It's content which very quickly becomes outdated, and once it's outdated, loses some of its usefulness and meaning.

When building content for your business, it's wise to include both types of content: solid principles you can continually refer back to as well as some timelier pieces dealing with the future, advances, or trends.

In terms of systematizing your business, evergreen content is going to be the best workhorse for creating and sustaining profitability.

One of the key areas I work with my business coaching clients on is in the area of evergreening their offers and sales content. This doesn't mean they have to sell the same thing forever, but it does mean that while they are selling something, they should set it up to make selling it as easy as possible.

This means to do a full and complete job, one time, of setting up the sales page, autoresponder, and product delivery and be able to reuse this same sales funnel each time they offer the same program, product or service.

So much time is wasted in continually creating new processes to sell the same thing. With a bit of forethought and some organization, you only need to create the infrastructure once, and you're able to profit from it over and over again. This is another kind of repurposing and another source of business leverage.

Sometimes the idea of selling the same thing in the same way over and over again feels boring to some clients. And I guess there is a difference, in my mind, between boring and consistent. In my opinion, I'd rather my money-making avenues be consistently producing for me, and I can find my excitement elsewhere.

This doesn't mean you can't add or change your sales process—of course you can. Add in videos, if you want to do videos. Bring in guest speakers if you want to. All that is fine—innovating your approach is good. Always be testing to see what works best. That's not what I'm talking about when I say you want to be consistent.

I'm advocating that you find ways to make your launches easier and smoother. One way to do this is by systematizing your content for these launches as much as you can. You can add on or tweak, but reduce the time spent on creating new campaigns from scratch for each launch of the same product or service.

Marketing is when your content meets other people.

The faster you can get your sales funnel in place each time you launch a program or service, the faster you can get to making money from your launch, rather than losing time in writing a new sales letter each time or new autoresponders each time.

You can do the same kind of template for your preview calls and definitely for your discovery sessions. Look for ways to re-use, repurpose, and retain your content so as to reduce the strain and huge workload that often seems to overshadow program or service launches.

CONTENT SYNDICATION

The final section of this chapter deals with the distinction between content creation and content distribution. These are two separate business functions. Both are important.

Content creation is the process of idea generation and development. It is the process by which ideas move into finished work product—written, audio, video, or a combination of these.

Content creation is not marketing. It is a necessary first step to marketing. You can't market your content if you don't have content in the first place.

But technically speaking, marketing is not the act of writing the article. That is content creation. Marketing is when you distribute that article in some way, making it available for others to access and benefit from.

This is where most people drop the ball. They publish an article to their blog and count it as a marketing activity. Yet if nobody comes to their blog and reads the article, no effective marketing actually occurred.

Marketing is when your content meets other people. Not when your content *might* have a chance, potentially, of meeting other people.

Marketing is about getting that article or audio or video out into the world for people to read, listen to, or watch.

Most businesses do not have an effective content distribution system. They write a blog post and that's all. Maybe some of them share it on Facebook or Twitter, but for the most part, most businesses do not invest enough in distribution of their content, and so their content never makes a big difference for their business.

Content syndication is the process of distributing your content across the web. Distribution is about creating greater visibility.

A very simple content syndication system example is one where you publish content to your blog, and then your blog post is also pushed to Twitter, Facebook, and LinkedIn. You've syndicated to three platforms in this model.

You can set up larger and more complex syndication systems by increasing the number and kinds of sites to which your content is submitted.

We discussed repurposing earlier in this chapter, and I mentioned how you could convert your content to other formats. Each of these individual formats can be syndicated as well.

A general example might look something like this:

Blog post sent to Twitter, Facebook and LinkedIn.
▼
Blog post turned into audio and submitted to various podcast sites.
▼
Blog post turned into a video and submitted to various video sites.
▼

Blog post turned into a slideshow and submitted to various slideshow sites.

▼

Blog post content sent to other remote blogs on other platforms.

▼

Blog post content converted to PDF and submitted to the document sharing sites.

And so on.

There are hundreds of places where your blog post could be submitted, and you can probably see that sharing your content on 100 relevant sites would create bigger results than having your content on just one site, right?

Content syndication is the process of taking your information and putting it out across the Internet, building a type of spider web, leading visitors back to the center of the web, which is your main website or blog.

Again, not every piece of content needs to be repurposed in every way and syndicated in every way. But your very best pieces of content have the potential to bring hundreds more people to your website simply through a process of thoughtful syndication.

Once you've mapped out a clear syndication strategy, you can rely on technology to help complete the syndication for you.

Creating great content, repurposing it and syndicating it are the three mainstays of a content strategy that can bring you ongoing results from a one-time effort. That is one powerful recipe for business leverage.

Chapter 14

GENERATING TRAFFIC

ONCE YOUR CONTENT is created and available, you're ready to start generating traffic.

Traffic, at the most basic level, is visitors to your website. I always recommend that you focus the bulk of your marketing towards getting visitors to your main website, one that you host and own. Yes, you can get visitors to your business Facebook page or Twitter account, but I believe doing that is building your business on shaky ground. Why spend all your time generating visitors to a page that you don't own? If Facebook were sold tomorrow, or Twitter closed down, and you've sent all your visitors to these sites, where would your business be?

This is why you want to build your authority website on your own domain name, on your own hosting.

There are two categories of traffic: targeted and untargeted. As they sound, targeted traffic is visitors who are interested in your topic and approach and who represent a potential base of future clients, colleagues, or business partners. Untargeted traffic is visitors who don't represent your future clients, colleagues, or business partners. They are people who somehow came to your site accidentally or randomly, sometimes through errant search engine listings. Untargeted traffic tends to leave your site very quickly, resulting in a high bounce rate.

One measure of your website's relevance and authority is in how many targeted visitors you attract and retain. Highly authoritative websites attract many visitors, and some percentage of those visitors frequently returns.

The important take away from this part of the chapter, so far, is that you want to generate targeted traffic. You can do this through the content you create and the distribution channels you employ.

Within the realm of targeted traffic, there are three subcategories representing various types of traffic. These three types of traffic are branded traffic, social traffic, and search traffic.

If you've installed and are using Google Analytics on your website, you will be accumulating a great deal of valuable information about who your visitors are and how they are finding you. In reviewing your Analytics, you will begin to see what proportion of your own website's traffic is branded, social, or search based.

Branded traffic is the type of traffic your site receives when people are doing searches for you by your name, company name, or product name. For most solo-entrepreneurs, branded traffic represents the biggest portion of the traffic they receive. When you review your Google Analytics, you will see searches for your name, company name, product name; these are all branded searches.

For instance, when I look in my Google Analytics, I see that I am getting visitors from Internet searches on "profitable popularity," "rachna jain," "rachna jain blog." These are all examples of branded traffic. They represent a group of people who has either met me in real life or online, or heard of me somehow directly from others. This represents the pool of people I am reaching directly through my existing business marketing. It may be directly from marketing I've done, or through marketing or mentions other people are doing for me—where they are recommending me by name to someone else.

Branded traffic tends to represent warmer business leads, meaning people who are a bit further into the discovery and sales process. Given that they have somehow heard about you and are inclined to seek you out to learn more, we can presume they are more interested in you and your business than people who aren't searching specifically for you. Branded traffic is good traffic to have, with the main downside being that it runs almost fully on your own energy, resources, and availability.

Branded traffic comes from people who you are speaking with directly. People who you are on teleseminars with. People who you are meeting at events and so on. Branded traffic is wonderful because it's a way of growing your reach and influence. When people are coming to your site after searching for your name or programs, it's their way of saying, "Yes, I met her. Yes, I've heard of him. S/he was wonderful. I want to learn more." The problem is in how challenging it can be to balance growing your site visitors, providing service, and doing all of the networking at the same time. Have you seen that as you get busier, some of your marketing starts to go downhill? The challenge with branded traffic is the minute you stop going to networking events, maybe speaking a little bit less on teleseminars, you have fewer people knowing of you and hearing about you and that tends to make people not come to your website so they can't sign up for your email list and so on.

Let's say you speak at four large events in one year. You write three articles for well-known blogs. You hold one teleseminar. All of these will result in an increase in your branded traffic. And that's good.

But what happens in year two, when you aren't able to speak at as many events? Or your articles don't get published as widely? Or your teleseminar has lower interest? You're very likely to see your branded traffic—and as a result, your overall website traffic—decrease significantly. The problem with branded traffic is that it stops working when you do. You have to constantly be actively marketing yourself in order to continue to benefit from branded traffic. When you get too busy to market, your visitors drop, and this can keep you stuck in the "feast or famine" cycle of entrepreneurship.

I see branded traffic as vitally important, but if that is your only source of traffic, you're missing out on the opportunity to make your business grow faster and more easily, with less work.

Now let's look at the second type of traffic: social traffic. As it sounds, this is traffic that comes from your participation in social media, most likely the social networks (Facebook, Twitter, LinkedIn). As an aside, these social networks represent only one of the eleven platforms of social media, but most people believe that social networks are all of social media. In this case, what you don't know may be hurting you. There are several social media technologies which can help you grow your business, but most people are not using them correctly, if they are even using them at all.

Social traffic is a few steps further down the continuum of traffic. It represents the direct contact and effort you make on the social networks, and as such, can be considered a type of branded traffic as well. Why I've chosen to separate it out from branded traffic is because social traffic now also has implications for improved search engine ranking.

If you think of a straight line, you can see traffic sources are on a continuum (see Fig. 14-1)—with branded traffic on one end, social traffic in the middle, and search engine traffic on the other end.

Social traffic is a generally warmer type of traffic like branded traffic, and again, you have to do the work yourself. You have to find or create engaging content, post your updates, and interact. Generally, social traffic tends to occur in spikes, as it's directly tied to something you've said or done. It does not tend to be as

BRANDED TRAFFIC   SOCIAL TRAFFIC   SEARCH TRAFFIC

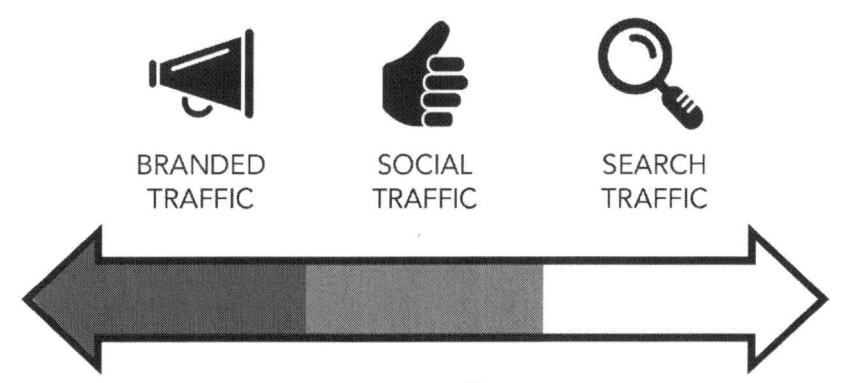

FIGURE 14-1: Traffic Continuum

long lasting as branded traffic or search traffic. It is also impacted by time-shift, meaning that not everyone will see your message at the same time, or even, perhaps, at all. To generate ongoing social traffic, you have to repeat yourself many times to be heard, and you need to repeat yourself multiple times on each individual social network.

One way of understanding this is that traditional marketing wisdom suggests that people need multiple exposures to your message before they take action on it. Traditional marketing suggests that people need seven contacts before they act. This is not always true, of course, especially if the offer is very compelling and very time sensitive, but for the most part, people will need at least a few exposures to your message to do anything about it.

In traditional direct response marketing, the marketer could control the rate and frequency of contact by sending out advertisements on a defined schedule. They could plan and time exactly when the target audience would receive their mailings or promotions.

This is not the case in social media because it is time-shifted and platform shifted. What time-shifted means here is that you, as the marketer, can't control the rate and frequency of contact. This has shifted to your target audience, as they decide when they check Twitter, when they check Facebook, and when they check LinkedIn. If they change their patterns, such as not logging in for several days, they are likely to miss your messages entirely. It is unlikely that everyone goes back to the start of their social network feed when they've missed several days. So some people are seeing your message once, some twice, some more than that, and some not at all. Social media is time-shifted for you as a marketer because you have no way of knowing for sure who has seen your message and when. The second aspect is that social media is platform shifted. Your target audience is using social networks from their smartphones, their tablets, and their home computers. Depending on where they are viewing social media from, they may be more or less inclined to review external links or long form content.

Suppose you create a marketing video for your newest program. You put this video on Facebook. If your target audience is logged into Facebook from their home computer, they may be open to viewing your video. If, however, your target audience is logging in via their smartphones, the screen size of their phone may make video viewing difficult. They may not be in a quiet place, so they can't hear your video well. They may not want to interrupt people around them, so they don't play your video. Do you see how this can impact your marketing?

One other challenge with social network marketing is that you also can't know how many people are able to access your messages. With some recent shifts in the Facebook algorithm, for example, I've noticed the pattern of my Facebook newsfeed has changed. I see a lot of updates from some people and hardly any from others. Sure, I can go and physically view their pages or purposefully and specifically subscribe to their updates, but in general, most people are not going to take this extra step in any kind of meaningful number.

Given that social traffic is both time and platform shifted, this can have direct impact on how many times your message is seen. And if your message is seen less, it will be acted upon less.

The third and final type of traffic is search traffic. It comes from the search engines, usually Google. Search traffic tends to enable you to be in front of people who are looking for what you are offering, but they don't know you by name. So it represents a larger opportunity and an untapped opportunity. It is people who want what you are selling, but they do not know you by name.

As I said, search traffic represents website visitors generated from your search engine ranking. This type of traffic tends to be colder traffic, meaning they are more cautious and less likely to immediately purchase. They are people who might be interested in purchasing what you offer, but they aren't sure yet. For this group especially, your site needs to educate and inform. The benefit of search traffic is that it doesn't rely solely on your efforts. It is a traffic source which can send you visitors 24 hours per day, 7 days per week, 365 days per year, without you having to constantly create and produce and share something new. This type of traffic is often the most underutilized in the businesses I've worked with.

When I review the traffic statistics for most businesses, what I see is an overload on branded traffic, some social traffic, and little to no search traffic.

Let me show you in a graphic.

This is what your business traffic most likely looks like:

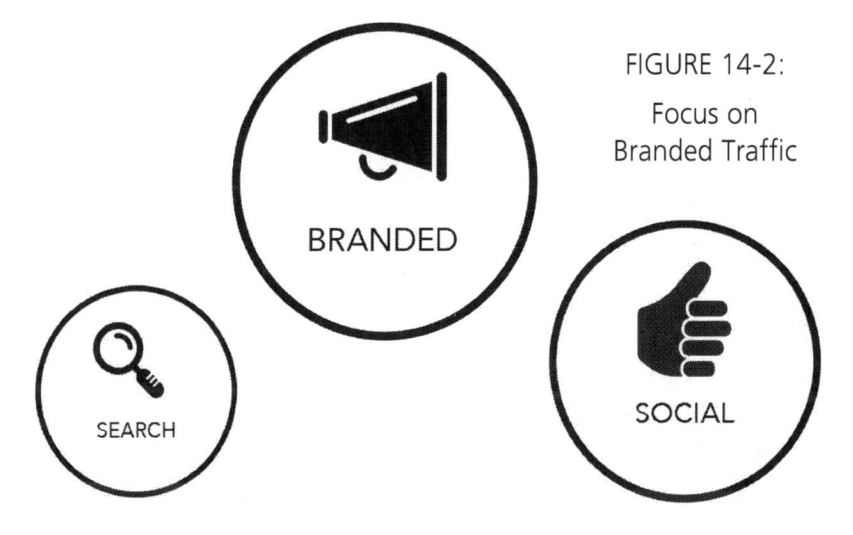

FIGURE 14-2: Focus on Branded Traffic

From this graphic, you can see that the bulk of your visitors are coming from work you're directly doing. You can see the graphic is a little uneven, heavily loaded towards branded and some to social, with almost no search.

For me, I've built my business mostly like this:

FIGURE 14-3: Focus on Search Traffic

Again, you can see the graphic is uneven, light on branded, some to social, big on search.

But what about a business that looks like this:

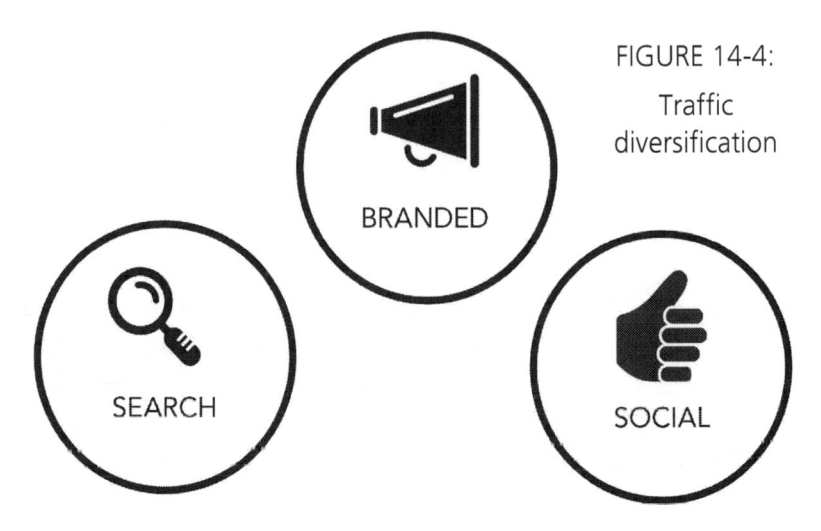

FIGURE 14-4: Traffic diversification

What would a business look like if you had big branding, big social and big search? Take everything that you are already doing to build your business and you add on this whole possibility of more social and more search. Search traffic runs for you all the time. Can you see that freed from having to do all the work yourself to bring visitors, you could then have more time and energy to focus on other areas? Search traffic can help you build a bigger business more easily.

As I see it, the key to being successful with traffic is to adopt a strategy of intelligent traffic diversification.

What this means is that you focus on building branded, social, and search traffic, so that you are growing your reach and stabilizing your client inflow.

While people seem to inherently understand the value of branded and social traffic, they seem less open to search traffic.

Two objections I often get about search traffic are these: "What I offer is very unique; I don't believe people are searching for me online." And "How do I know these people coming from the search engines will be my people?"

Let's address the first objection. I know you have a unique offering; hopefully you've positioned yourself as a category of one. But even though you offer something unique, there is a word or two or three that would define your group of offerings. What is the result you help people achieve? That is what you would use to see if people are looking for your kinds of services online. One of the ways that you begin to drive traffic is you begin to look at how people are looking for you. The way that the search engines run, the way that you start to target words for the search engines is with a concept called Search Volume. Search Volume refers to how many people are searching for a particular word or phrase. It would be people who are searching for a particular outcome or a certain kind of professional help, such as how many people are searching for weight loss, coach, weight loss coaching, lose weight—something like that.

When we look at Search Volume, it tells us a couple of things. It tells us how big the market is, how many people are looking. We can also find how competitive the market would be to start targeting that key word.

If you want to try this out for yourself, here's how to begin.

Start by taking the next 30 seconds and jotting down 5 or 6 phrases, two or three word phrases that people may use to find someone like you.

Once you have these phrases, you can see how many people are searching for them.

Google offers a free keyword tool which will give you a beginning sense of how large the market is that is searching on the words you wrote down. It's a good place to begin. For a full scale search engine optimization campaign, you'd want to use other keyword sources than just this one, but I offer this as a way of opening the door and helping you see what's possible.

To find the search volume on your terms, you can either go to Google and type in "Google Keyword Tool" or use this direct link: http://adwords.google.com/o/KeywordTool

Or if it's easier, I set up a link that you can use to go there directly:

The link is http://www.profitablepopularity.com/go/googlekt. The Google KT stands for Google Keyword Tool.

When you go to that page, you'll see a screen that asks you to enter your keywords. If you have a free Adwords account, you will get more complete results if you sign in using that. But if you just want to get the feel of how to do this, you don't need to sign in.

In the center part of the screen, you'll see a white box that asks you to list your keywords. These are the 5-6 phrases you just jotted down. Enter the word phrases you came up with into the box. Complete the captcha and hit search.

After a few seconds, you'll get a list of keywords. You will see the ones you entered appearing in this list, as well as others. These others are keywords Google sees as related to your main search query.

In this view, if you look to the right of the keywords, you'll see several columns. One of them is global search volume. This tells you how many people searched this term, worldwide, in the past 30 days.

For example, if you were to go to the Keyword Tool and type in Weight Loss Coaching, you will see that the general market is about 1,900 searches per month. This means that each month, 1,900 people are searching for the words "weight loss coaching" or some related variants in the search engines.

These are people who are exploring their specific service options. They don't know of someone directly, perhaps, and they are looking online for someone to help them. Now, if you offer a service that helps people reduce their weight, wouldn't you want to be in front of these people who are looking for more information on this type of service?

I would.

The next factor to review is the competition level. Google gives you a broad idea of how many other websites are competing for ranking on that same phrase. Competition can be low, medium, or high. Low means that there are fewer websites trying to rank for that term. High means that the term has a lot of competition.

Generally speaking, unless you are investing in expert SEO services, you want to locate and target lower competition words and word phrases. These are likely to be easier to rank for, and because they are easier to rank for, are likely to bring you new visitors more quickly. In general, you want to target low competition words with around 1,000 searches per month, and these words should be relevant and related to what you do. There is more to the process of keyword research than I've outlined here, but this will at least help you begin the process.

One other point I want to raise here is the issue of rightsizing your search volume to match your business objectives. If you do a few keyword searches, you will find that some keywords are getting 300,000 or more searches per month. If you're still thinking that bigger is better, you might be tempted to go for these types of keyword phrases, especially when you see the competition is low.

Don't do it.

Usually, words with such high search volume and low competition are not actually specific enough to represent good qualified leads for your business. As I mentioned already, people use the Internet for many purposes. They sometimes go online to gather information, sometimes to read reviews, and sometimes to make a purchase. The way that searchers use the Internet can be overlaid onto a buying continuum. People who are just gathering information on something are farthest away on the continuum; they represent the non-buying end. People who are reading reviews are likely further down the continuum, closer to making a purchase. People who are very close to purchasing tend to use very specific words and to search tightly. They are not using words like "weight loss"; they are using words like "weight loss program" or "online weight loss program" or "weight loss coach in Los Angeles."

This concept has to do with buyer intent and is important when you are reviewing search volume.

GATHERING INFORMATION   READING REVIEWS   SEARCHING TIGHTLY

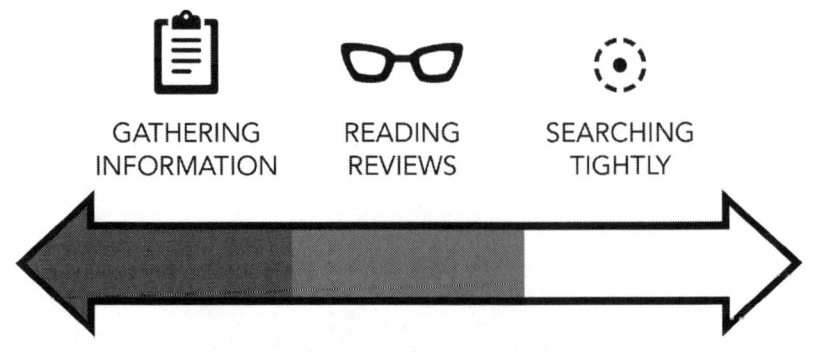

FIGURE 14-5: Buyer intent continuum

If you go after a really widely searched and non-specific keyword, like weight loss, and are able to rank for it, you are likely to get a lot of visitors, but many of them will simply click off your site because they are in the stage of looking for information and perhaps not quite ready for a solution.

If your site offers good information that is relevant to their concerns, you have a chance of capturing their interest—this is why I suggest an authority site approach to building your website content. With more authoritative and relevant content on your site, you have a greater chance of converting each visitor to an interested prospect.

One last point about rightsizing your search volume relates to your business objectives. If you are a solo professional, for instance, you will have an upper limit on how many clients you can accept in a particular time frame. If you only want to work with 12 clients, once you reach 12, you have no way to deal with overflow, unless you are willing to hire someone or contract with someone to take your overflow work. So one thing I do when working with clients and helping them find keywords is to try to match the search volume to their business model.

If I am working with someone who wants a small, boutique business as I have, they can't benefit from and therefore don't need, immense search volume. For them, perhaps even 50-100 new targeted visitors per month would be beneficial, especially if their site was able to convert two or three of these 50-100 people into new clients each month. Do you see what I mean? If you want to have a small, boutique business, you need fewer clients each month, so you don't need to invest in gaining high search engine ranking on hundreds of highly searched terms.

If, on the other hand, I'm working with someone who wants to build a larger platform, such as for a book launch or information product, then we look at terms with higher search volume. If you are offering a product that doesn't really have a limitation on supply (you can always print more books or always take more people into your membership program), you can seek either more highly searched terms or to gain ranking on many more lower searched terms, and your business can benefit from all these extra visitors.

When I work with a client who wants to do both, perhaps offer high level or platinum level packages and to build a larger platform for product sales, we tend to focus on both kinds of keywords. I try to help them achieve ranking on the lower competition words first, so they get some faster return on their investment with me. Then over time, I help them gain ranking on more competitive or more highly searched terms. Remember, if you are building authority, there is a cumulative effect. If you gain ranking on less searched, less competitive terms first, this often acts as stepping stones to gaining ranking on higher searched, more competitive terms later.

If you spend some time testing out different keywords, you will likely begin to understand, as I do, that yes, indeed, people are searching for your type of services online—no matter how unique your approach or delivery method. The key to this is thinking about the results they are seeking and using this as a beginning framework to build some keyword sets for your particular business.

So that, I hope, addresses the first objection of whether people are searching for your services online. They most likely are.

Let's look at the second objection—are these people my people? Will they buy from me?

After people spend some time reviewing search volume and competition, their next question often goes something like this: "OK, Rachna, I believe you. People are looking online for the type of service I offer. But how do I know they are MY people?" And my answer is that we don't. There is no way to know with 100% certainty that they will buy from you. Nobody can make that claim or know that for sure. But what we do know is that they are seeking the results you provide and are likely to be interested in knowing about you, especially if you have a proven process that can solve their problems. What we're basically looking to do is give your business an opportunity to be considered as one possible solution to their current area of concern.

One of the biggest objections people have to search marketing is in believing that these people searching are not likely to invest. And that is true, in a way, as not all searchers are looking to buy right now. People use Internet searches to gather information, and to learn about their options, and may not be ready to make a decision right away.

However, it is inaccurate to believe they never will. In fact, as I might have already alluded to, I've built a six-figure plus coaching business purely from search engine traffic. I've shared details of that with you in the Case Studies chapter. Once you read that, you'll see that yes, definitely, your people will invest with you.

In the past, it used to be that you could rely solely on single sources of traffic and still have a viable and growing business. This is no longer the case, and the wise entrepreneur invests in intelligent traffic diversification.

Intelligent traffic diversification is a term I use to describe the acquisition of website visitors from multiple sources, so that your site gains in ranking, authority, and reputation. When you create multiple sources of traffic, you are less dependent on any one source of traffic, which now is a very good thing. When you focus on generating branded, social, and search engine visitors, you will create a powerful and useful balance of immediate benefit and long term value.

Building a business based purely on branded and/or social traffic will become exhausting, as you are constantly driving the business forward on your own shoulders. If you stop meeting people or speaking at events, your website visitors will also decrease. Building a business purely from search traffic usually takes between six to nine months, as it takes some time to achieve search engine ranking and then some time to educate and persuade your visitors to buy. This doesn't mean that you'll be ranking for all your desired keyword terms in this time frame, but you will begin to see visitors coming from the search engines in this time frame. If you are looking to build a strong search engine presence, it is wise to plan to invest between six to twelve months in parallel to the other branded and social marketing you are already doing.

The most solid business foundation is built on using all three kinds of traffic: branded, social, and search. That way, if one of these declines, you still have the other two working for you.

In a long term view, generating branded, social, and search traffic will enable you to build a profitable asset in your business. Not only will these strategies bring in a return for you now, but eventually, you might be able to sell your business and/or website for high dollar because of all the targeted visitors it receives. If you like, consider your website as a piece of virtual real estate, with the capacity to appreciate and grow in value as long as, like a physical home, you take care of curb appeal, and make sure it's functional and beautiful for those who use it.

Your next step is to focus on deeply learning or deeply committing to just three to five ways to generate website visitors, making sure you have at least one strategy coming from each of the categories of branded traffic, social traffic, and search traffic.

Using this method, you'll be able to attract more opportunities and more dollars.

You will become more well-known and make more money more easily.

Chapter 15

BUILDING YOUR AUTHORITY WEBSITE

ONE OF THE slow and steady growth strategies I recommend to my clients is that they seek to build their profile and credibility through the process of building an authority website.

As it sounds, an authority website is a "go-to" website in its niche. It offers relevant, useful, and original content and is well optimized for all three kinds of traffic.

With all the recent changes in online and search marketing, I have become more convinced that building an authority website is the best way to build your online presence for long term success.

Building a website that is an authority in its niche can take some time to achieve, and the effort is well worth it.

To my way of thinking, a website becomes an authority when it possesses several key characteristics.

First, it is well designed and well optimized, both for the visitor and the search engines. For most service businesses, it should include a picture and/or video of you, the service provider/owner on the front page.

You want a clean design, well marked with descriptive navigation. One page that is often missing from service business websites is a "work with me" or "hire me" page. Make sure your site includes this page.

Also be sure to include a contact form or contact page directly on your site. Make the home page striking, and use a decent amount of copy on the page.

The home page copy should include information about what you do and should describe the results you help your clients achieve.

Don't be so quick to send your site visitors off to your social media profiles. Once they are on your site, you want them to stay for a while.

Create a visitor pathway that directs them to what you want them to do first, second, and third. This might be something along the lines of asking them to sign up for your email newsletter, watch a certain video, and then leave you a comment.

Give people a pathway to follow so they know how to learn more about you.

Be sure to include anything that helps build your authority or credibility. Your "About Me" page should include a picture of you (yes, again!) and some information about your background, training, experience. Try to include client testimonials and/or case studies on your site. (I include both on mine.) These can give potential clients a strong understanding of what you do and the results you create.

A site that is well designed and well optimized creates a positive experience for the visitor, and that can translate into improved search engine positioning as well, given that the search engines appear to factor how long visitors remain on your site as one component in assigning search engine ranking.

An authority website is relevant and timely. The content reads well and has been updated recently. This doesn't mean that you're changing your main website each day. But be sure that you review or update it at least once every six months, so it has a freshness and relevance to it.

Your authority website should also include a blog. There is much debate about whether to put your blog on the same domain or on a different domain. In almost all cases, I recommend having it on your main domain. My reasoning for this is that all the content you put on your blog then accrues value to your main business domain, which is what you want to have happen.

Also, frankly, if it's on your main domain, you're more likely to update your blog more regularly. It's not worth starting a blog if you aren't willing to maintain it.

If you're not able to post as often as you'd like, then remove the dates on your blog posts. Nothing screams "lack of attention" when a new site visitor goes to your blog and sees that your last post was made five months ago. It's not uncommon for them to wonder if you're still in business.

Blogging is the best way I know to build ranking and authority.

Sites are ranked in the search engines by a combination of several factors. As a site owner, many of these are in your control. On your site itself, the important factors include the topic of the site and whether the content matches the site and is relevant. Sites which have a topic and content match meet the first level of criteria for ranking. If the sites are easy to navigate, well optimized on the technical side (using elements like title tags, meta descriptions, and keywords), then they pass the second level of criteria for ranking.

Once these factors are in place, the next criteria to determine ranking comes from how many—and what kinds—of sites link into yours. While a full review of search engine optimization is outside the scope of this book, a basic overview is likely to be helpful.

In order to build an authority website, you must have a wide variety of good and valuable sites linking into yours. When site A links to your site, it will often do this through a clickable (hyperlinked) URL. When the search engine sees that site A is linking to you, it counts that one URL as a backlink (as in a link back to your site from site A).

The backlink is considered a sign of trust or endorsement—similar to introducing one colleague to another at a networking event. In this case, site A is saying to its website visitors, "Hey, you might want to check out this other site too." This acts as an endorsement for your website, as measured by the backlink.

Generally speaking, the sites which have good content, are well optimized, have good internal linking across their own pages, are regularly updated, are on topic and relevant, and also have a number of good and valuable backlinks coming into them are the ones that get the most visits. When they get the most visits, they are also seen as more authoritative—so authority begets more authority.

The reason I'm spending so much time here is because most people do not take such a long term view of their website and blog. They blog because they feel they should, but they don't really understand why.

Blogging on a regular basis builds your immediate authority and presence because people know who you are and what you have to say. It also has long term benefits, where the more relevant content you publish, the more likely you are to have some of the content referenced by other sites and to create backlinks.

Backlinks are also created when content is shared in the open social media platforms, such as Twitter, Pinterest, and on your Facebook business page. In this description, an open platform is one where people can view the content without signing in to the site. Examples of non-open platforms would be your Facebook personal profile and LinkedIn profile.

Open access is important for backlinks to be found and counted. Part of search engine optimization includes the gaining of these off-site links coming into your site.

While there are many ways to gain these, some common ones are through writing articles for online sites or magazines, guest blogging on other blogs, social bookmarking good content, submitting your site to blog directories and web directories, document sharing, slideshows, and video marketing. All of these, done correctly, will accomplish the two-fold purpose of building awareness of your site and content while building valuable backlinks to your site at the same time.

When I first began my business, I believed that search engine ranking was the absolute best way to build your business. You'll see in my case study of my dissertation site (see the Case Studies chapter later in this book), that I built this site purely from content and search marketing.

This website has multiple high rankings in the search engines on multiple terms. Each term sends me visitors who come from searching for a term or phrase which appears on my site, finding my site listing in the search engines, and clicking through to learn more.

The only job of the search engines is to put your site in front of people who are looking for what you sell.

Once they click through to your site, the goal of your site is to help them decide if your business is what they are looking for. It's impossible for your site to meet everyone's needs, so you will get a certain amount of visitors who come to your site and immediately leave. (This is bounce rate, which we discussed in the metrics chapter.) Every site that uses search marketing does get some bounce rate. If the bounce rate is too high, it can mean that either your marketing is not targeting the right people, or that your website content isn't compelling enough. It might also mean that you're getting visits from terms you're ranking for randomly—that is, ones you're not actively targeting.

Once someone is on your website and feels that you might be able to help them, the next thing they will often do is either contact you directly or try to sign up for something free to learn more about you. This free offering might be your newsletter, some training videos, or perhaps a teleclass or webinar you're offering.

It's a good idea to have something free like this available on your site. Depending on how rapidly you want to build connection and how deeply you want to get their attention, you might consider offering an audio or video rather than an ecourse or electronic report. The reason for this is that audio and video tend to build intimacy faster and can accelerate the process of connection and relationship building with people who are coming to know of you for the first time.

Be sure to make it easy to subscribe to your free offering; make the free offer prominent and attention getting when someone first comes to your site. Be sure to test various kinds of free offers, as well. This is one way of collecting specific data about what kinds of free offers in your business will draw the best response.

No matter what your main free offer is, it's also wise to consider how you will move people from your free offering to the first paid offer. This is why having a clear sales funnel and a planned upgrade path is useful. There is no purpose in having thousands of people on your email list if you are unable to activate them to ever purchase anything. Remember, we don't want to cultivate friends, fans, or followers for the sake of numbers. For our business profitability, we want to cultivate people who will buy.

When you are building content for your authority website, you have a few options of the kinds of content to include. For the most part, you want content that is 100% original and longer in length. Short posts are fine occasionally, but not all the time. Your content should be focused around a particular topic or group of topics and should seek to accomplish several objectives.

First, it should be interesting and entice the visitor to keep reading. Focus on topics your visitors will likely care about. Keep your posts and articles within your identified topical area.

Second, express an opinion. Your blog and content is a way to establish the foundation of your thought leadership. The idea here is to find ways to answer questions, address problems, and give your expert advice and suggestions for addressing the challenges your website visitors might be facing.

Third, your content should build your reputation. It should position you in a way that you attract more opportunities in your industry or field. A well-written blog is, like a book, a strong credibility builder.

If you take the time to write strong content and take the time to syndicate it, as we touched on in the chapter on traffic, you will naturally attract more opportunities and invitations.

For instance, from my writing alone, I've been invited to speak at live events and on teleseminar and webinar series. My writing has attracted guest blogging and republishing inquiries and has also generated interviews in major print and online media.

This is why you want to build an authority website and authoritative presence online. The work you invest in doing this will reward you with an ongoing stream of new opportunities to share your business and your expertise.

Recall how I said that the most authoritative sites were optimized for search traffic, social traffic, and branded traffic?

We've already touched on how to think about optimizing for search. To optimize for branding, be sure to name your programs and pages consistently to match how you present them when speaking with other people. So if you name your program "3 Ways to Save Money in Your Business," make sure this is the title of your website page too. This way, people who type in what they remember hearing have a good chance of finding you.

If you have an unusual name that is commonly misspelled, try to also register the misspellings of your name. This came up for me recently when someone finally found me, but only after typing "rashnajane" and variations of that in order to search me out.

I actually own my name: rachnajain.com—but it never occurred to me that people would be spelling it purely phonetically. I've since registered rashnajane.com and redirected it to my main site.

Now granted, I have no way of knowing for sure how many people are spelling my name this way. But I figured that $8 per year for a domain name wasn't a lot to invest to try to be in front of people who are looking for me.

While we're on the subject of domain names, make sure you register your own domain name and retain ownership of it all along. I have had clients who register their domains through other services and then must "buy out" the domain when they leave the service contract.

The same way you wouldn't give someone the deed to your physical residence to hold for you, don't give them your domain name which is, essentially, the "deed" to your virtual home.

When you are optimizing for branded traffic, it's also wise to include the names of events in your page content as well. If you attend a live event and speak, do add something about this live event to your website, so that people who type in your name with the title of the event and/or with the name of the organizer of the event can find you also. Even though you will have provided your URL in your talk and even though attendees may have collected your business card, it doesn't always mean they will refer to these items when they are sitting at the computer and want to connect with you.

If you want to optimize for social traffic (that is, traffic coming from social media), you want to be sure to have social sharing buttons for your content. Make these visible and easy to locate. Don't expect, though, that simply putting these on your site will be enough to encourage people to share. Sometimes they will, of course. But don't be hesitant to encourage sharing by asking readers to share. It never hurts to ask, especially if your content is good and worth sharing.

The most important element of building an authority site is consistency over time. The sites which create a positive user experience, generate strong, diversified traffic, and are mentioned in social media are the sites which are doing the best overall in terms of building attention and generating buzz.

The sites which have a business model for turning this attention into dollars are the ones which are most profitable.

Again, your goal in building an authority website is to position yourself as an expert. To attract new opportunities. To shorten your sales cycle. To attract new clients. To, perhaps, position yourself as a thought leader, and from that, maybe leave a legacy.

When you tie your activities of marketing into the larger framework of how they will benefit your business, they suddenly start to make more sense and encourage more effort and consistency.

If I know that writing a good blog post today will generate some good opportunities for me in the future, I'm always more motivated to write a good blog post. When you don't understand that building your online presence in this way can create benefits now and into the future, you feel disconnected about why you're posting to your blog.

It's this disconnection between your actions and their outcomes which makes it more difficult to maintain the discipline and consistency required to run and grow a successful business.

NOTES

Chapter 16

YOUR CONTENT MONEY SPIRALS

NOW THAT WE'VE reviewed the first two circles in the Profitable Popularity method, content and traffic, it's time to take a look at the third: monetization. This means we will be looking at ways to make money from your content.

The way I see it is that content leads to money, and money leads to content. There is a reciprocal relationship.

There is what I call a "content-money" spiral which we'll talk about in just a bit. Prior to that, though, I want to start at the very simplest part of the spiral, a very direct monetization method that most people can grasp.

The most direct way that your content makes money can be seen when you accept advertising on your blog. Your blog content has generated enough visitors and enough interest that someone wants to pay you to advertise on your blog.

Yes, there are specific networks for this and you can go that route, but if you take the time to create good content and distribute it regularly, your readership will rise. As your readership rises, you will automatically be sought out by people looking to advertise on your site.

To me, this is the simplest and most direct example of how words on your page can put money in the bank.

Advertising is one way to turn content into money. Another way is by adding affiliate links to your content.

In this second example, you might write about a particular software product that helps solve a problem in your business, and at the end of that article, you might include your affiliate link to the software. An affiliate link means that you will receive some kind of payment or compensation if someone purchases the software after clicking on your link.

Affiliate links are a second way to make money from your content. I see them as more active than advertising, and you'll see that the money-making methods become more specific and more individual as we proceed.

The reason I bring both of these monetization methods up is two-fold. First, they are easy to understand. Most of us have seen advertising on websites and we understand, inherently, that these advertisements want us to purchase something. From the world of traditional newspapers and journals, we understand that the advertiser has paid to place their ad, and we have no difficulty understanding how this translates to the Internet as well.

Even though affiliate income is a slightly more advanced topic, it is easy to understand. When I say advanced, I don't mean it in the placement of the link itself, but instead, within the idea of being able to sell someone else's program, products, or services through your recommendation. There are guidelines around transparency and having to disclose that you are making a recommendation for which you will be compensated.

The first reason I include both is they provide a baseline for grasping how content leads to money. The second reason I include them is because they, very often, can supplement and add to the more specific monetization we'll be looking at next. In essence, they can contribute some additional incremental income to your business from content you were creating anyway and which may not have a specific business monetization focus in place already.

You can use advertising and affiliate links on your site to monetize content that is not designed to lead someone to a program, product, or service offering of yours.

As we begin to look at how content creates money in a more specialized way, let's begin with an example.

When you create a program, you create content in an organized way in order to deliver that program. You create the program itself; that's one large chunk of content. Then, as you deliver the program, you receive questions from the participants. In answering these questions, you have more ideas and more content to add to the course. Participants may share stories, may make comments, may give suggestions for what else you might include or that you might cover. All of these create more content that you can use to make more money.

The content-monetization process is a spiral, where each new type of content can generate new promotional or service options.

Let me show you just one "slice" of this kind of spiral. See Figure 16:1 on top of page 222.

Let's start with a blog post. You write your blog post and put it on your blog.

Eventually, you have enough blog posts that you can gather them by themes, organize them, and you can create an ebook.

You can give your ebook away to generate email subscribers, or you can sell it. Let's say you decide to sell it, since we are talking about monetization. So now, you have this ebook available to sell.

In the ebook, you've strategically decided that you want to create conversations with people who purchase the ebook, so you include questions throughout the ebook and invite people to submit their most burning questions to you and in return, you invite them to a Q&A session or teleseminar.

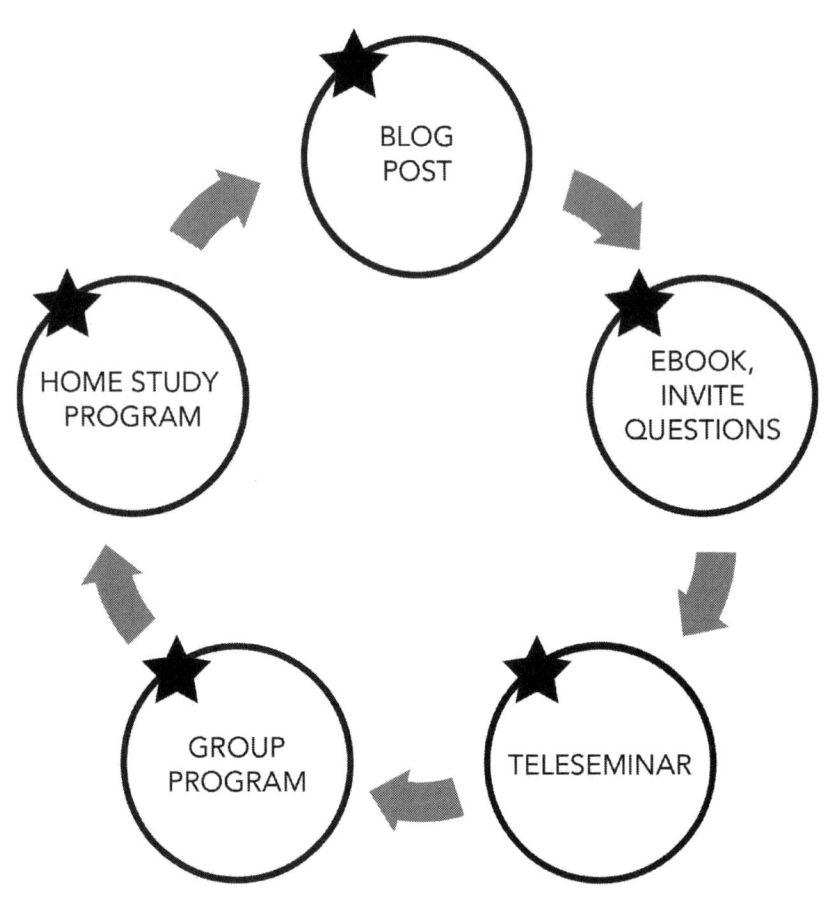

FIGURE 16:1: Content-Monetization Spiral

You invite them to submit their questions and to join your teleseminar waiting list, so they can be invited when the teleseminar is ready.

So then you have gathered a list of possible teleseminar participants. You host the Q&A call, and then, on the Q&A call, you invite them to go deeper with you, perhaps in the form of a group coaching program based on the topic of the ebook.

When you host the group coaching, you record the sessions, perhaps for a home study program. And then, again, you have audios you can either share for free, or which you can sell. If you choose to sell them, your content can, again, open up another stream of money.

In the graphic of this spiral slice, you'll see that some of the items are starred. This is the content, and it's starred because you can use it to either make money or send traffic, or you can, with some content adjusting, do both.

Let's say that you have 100 people reading your blog post. 50 of them buy your ebook. 25 of them submit questions and attend your Q&A session. Out of the 25 who attend, five or six sign up for your group coaching program. So from a "free" blog post, you've made money on ebook sales, perhaps on the Q&A session if you charged for it, but even if you didn't, you again made money on the sales of the group coaching program.

The cycle of offering something free (blog post) leading to something paid (ebook) leading to something free (Q&A call) leading to something paid (group coaching program) is a good example of the ways that content can be free but can lead to money AND of how content can be paid for, and that obviously creates money as well.

Most entrepreneurs do not take the time to create this kind of content/monetization flow in their business. Instead, they view each item as distinct and residing in its own bucket (mini-Universe) in their business. They treat each product or service as an isolated event, not seeing how each can flow into the next. They end up with a wide variety of products, but perhaps, only sell a few copies of each a year. This is a waste. You can make much more money when you create a cycle of offerings where you can keep moving people more deeply into connection with you, as you keep creating more content that you can utilize in the future.

Let's continue with another slice of the spiral shown in Figure 16:2 on page 224, picking up from the group coaching program that you've turned into a home study program.

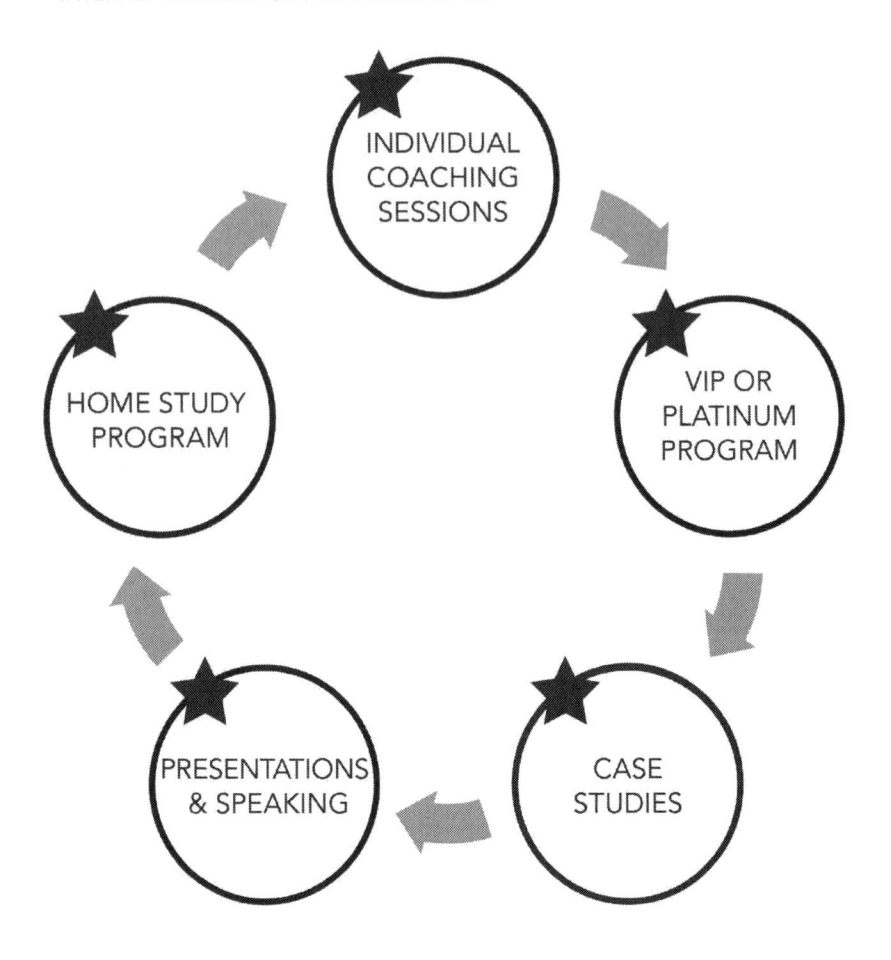

FIGURE 16:2: Content-Monetization Spiral 2

In this spiral slice, we pick up with the home study program. When people purchase your home study program, they also receive the opportunity to contact you for individual coaching sessions.

If they begin in individual coaching, you will create more ideas and can create more content. You may record the sessions with the client's permission and somehow use excerpts or pieces to giveaway or to sell.

These coaching sessions might generate more blog post ideas. I routinely get new ideas for blog posts from questions my clients ask in our coaching sessions. Then, if you have a new blog post, you can run it through the monetization spiral again.

But for now, let's return back to individual coaching. From these two or three individual sessions, you might invite them to join a VIP day or Platinum program.

From this VIP day or Platinum program, you can create case studies which you can use in your programs, sales pages, and speaking presentations.

You could sell your home study program at your speaking presentations, or group coaching, or individual sessions. Or you could simply build your email list from this opportunity, knowing you will have a way to stay in touch and perhaps sell something later.

If you grasp the concept of this content-money spiral, you'll see that you can work all the way up the spiral and all the way down the spiral. You can enter the spiral at any point and make a decision to monetize your content in some particular way.

You will make the most money if you use this spiral to focus on selling services rather than products. I love information products, don't get me wrong. It's just that they have a stronger likelihood of resulting in cycle breakage, where purchasers invest in a product, but never use it, and because they've never used the product, they don't feel they can invest more with you until they use the product.

So, in essence, selling products without some kind of service component attached will mean that you will have to make an effort to keep reaching new people because you'll have a higher percentage of people who have bought the first product, don't really use it or don't use it well, and they get kind of stuck there.

The other inherent piece of this is that you must have a simultaneous focus on building new contacts and gaining new subscribers even as you're developing your content-money spiral. I believe I raised this already in an earlier chapter, but it's vital that you keep growing your reach and email list alongside developing this monetization process. Otherwise, you run the risk of selling everything you can to everyone you know, and there comes a point where nothing more is selling because everyone who was interested has already purchased. This is the danger of a closed system in your business—one where you're not actively connecting with more people and increasing your group of people who might potentially purchase from you.

It's also vital to develop a monetization process and go deep rather than wide. This means that you commit to what you're selling, and you sell as much of it as you can. It's better to offer fewer items in your "store" and sell more of them, than it is to try to offer fifty or so items you can't easily support.

After all, if you're the main person responsible for service delivery after the sale, you want to have a life outside of work too.

The other recommendation I have is to build up your monetization streams in a thoughtful and considered way. Too often, people try to turn out huge projects which are not the next logical step in their business.

For example, as I think I've mentioned, I didn't begin actively cultivating a regular email newsletter for many years. This was a mistake on my part, so I want to warn against it. Anyway, because I didn't invest in this early on, my list is reasonably small relative to the size of my business and how long I've been working. My list growth has also been impacted by the fact that I worked for many years "behind the scenes" and didn't make much effort to be directly and personally visible.

In any case, what this means is that there are certain business approaches that don't make a lot of sense for me right now because I don't yet have enough reach and "fame" or "popularity" to make them work.

Let me give you a specific instance of this. I began this year with two goals in mind: the first was to hold a live event of my own, and the second was to write this book. I initially thought I'd hold the live event—that felt like it had more energy for me. But when I looked at the process of holding a live event, I realized that my current reach and client base was probably too small to support a live event of medium size. I stepped back from this goal and realized that it might make more sense to write my book first, see if that helped grow my visibility and popularity, and then perhaps, revisit the idea of a live event once I knew more people and they knew of me.

Don't overinvest in small, incremental streams of income at the expense of your larger, more sustainable ones.

Even though the live event felt exciting and energized, I realized that it wasn't the next logical step for my business because I didn't yet have all the resources in place to make it likely to succeed.

This is why, again, it's important to give some thought to your strategy and to the timing of your monetization. You want to use critical thinking and business clarity to identify what the logical next steps are for your business growth.

It makes me sad when I hear about new business owners who try to run huge launches or run a huge teleseminar series when they don't really have the infrastructure in place to fully benefit from this huge exposure. They spend months running themselves ragged trying to have this one big hit or rushing influx when, really, they could make money faster and in a more sustainable way if they focused smaller and used the concept of "What's my next logical step?"

If you don't know specifically how you expect a huge launch to make you money, that understanding is not going to suddenly appear while you're in the middle of it. When you are creating a money stream in your business, do it with care and thoughtfulness and commitment. Give yourself time to test and refine, time to think and grow, and invest fully—body, heart, mind, and soul—in whatever you choose to monetize in your business.

One other caution: don't invest too much time and effort in income streams which bring you too little money. I see this often in the area of membership sites/continuity programs. There is an illusory belief that running a membership site is passive income. That all you have to do is put the membership site together, and members will automatically join and stay.

Sounds good, right?

Unfortunately, it's not what usually happens.

Membership income is good income; it's nice to have. But to build it into a sustainable and significant source of business revenue requires work. It takes effort to build a sizable community. And even if your membership fee is low and the value of your site is very high, you are still asking people to commit on a monthly basis to being involved.

Each time the membership charge reaches their credit card, they run a mental check of whether it feels worth it to continue their subscription.

I'm not saying that this model can't work; I'm just saying that it's not as "passive" as you might think.

Don't overinvest in small, incremental streams of income at the expense of your larger, more sustainable ones.

And again, don't rush to productize your knowledge too quickly. We're wired to believe we can get all we need from buying programs and learning the material on our own. Yet we each have examples in our own life of how we buy programs and never use them.

Building income streams can sometimes require trial and error. When you have a good idea, you want to test it as rapidly as you can to see if people will invest in it. If they do, you have some data that this is what they want and will pay for. Don't get too caught up in any one idea without some proof—even a bit—that it will be something people will invest in. It makes no sense to build out a huge business plan or launch plan for a service or product when you have no concrete proof that people will actually buy.

There are many things people love and appreciate that they wouldn't necessarily invest in. Your main job is to find the intersection between what people love and appreciate AND what they would invest in.

It can be a fun, exploratory process if you let it be. The key is to not get so caught up in loving your idea until you see how the marketplace responds. Sometimes that response may be a bit slower than you'd like, so it's important to keep refining, testing, and tweaking. And don't give up too soon! As long as you're learning and gaining new information each time you make an offer, you're on the right track.

One last point: as you find something you love and others love and will buy, develop these income streams in a sustainable way.

The most money is made from easy to deliver income streams which are offered consistently. Again, it's that idea of digging deep and extracting all the value you can when you find a place that delivers. Success is a sign—you want to repeat what's working!

The flipside of this is that I don't believe it should always require a Herculean-type effort to make money in your business. If it does, it means that either the offer needs adjusting, the audience is wrong, or the mode of delivery needs to be looked at.

In many cases, you can discern the missing link faster through research and development, surveys, conversations, or mini-focus groups than you can sitting alone in your office trying to figure it out on your own.

It is possible to create money quickly. When there is alignment between what you offer and what your audience wants, money happens.

When you have been in business for a while, you will naturally see that your business services begin to evolve. Your clients' businesses will grow, and their needs will change. They will ask you for new services or products. If they are happy working with you, they will ask you first if you are able to meet their new needs.

When this happens, you have the opportunity to evolve your services to meet these new needs. You don't have to, of course, but often, evolution of your services can and does uplevel your business.

We all begin with an idea of what we sell, and then we see that this changes and transforms by the act of working with our clients. We see what services are most desired, which are less so, and we begin to adapt and adjust to make our businesses better match what clients need. It's an open, living system.

And, like any other open, living system, it is subject to change—and not just from external forces. Client needs may change, the working relationship may change, the industry may change.

Even though change can be difficult, being able to dance with change is another aspect of business resilience and agility.

One way I look at it in my business is by asking myself to try to find the opportunity in this change. Sometimes, it's a new service I can develop and offer. Other times, it is a new strategic partnership I can cultivate. And still other times, it is about finding a trusted provider of some service my clients need and want which I am not interested or equipped to provide.

This approach relies on keeping your clients' needs and your business needs moving forward together. You are always searching for that sweet spot where your clients' needs and your business needs intersect. You don't want to overvalue one to the other because that creates an imbalance that doesn't work. Rather, you want to find a way to match up together in a way that works for your clients and for you.

The one final note about making money is that you will make more money the more you can get help in your business.

I never really understood this until this past year, when I went through a phase of extreme revenue growth and found that my best plans and systems were not adequate to keep up with the flow of new business coming to me.

The flow of new business happened rapidly, beginning immediately after a speaking engagement where I received 52 discovery session requests. I was not prepared for this rapid influx, and my business systems began to crumble under the strain. Until that time, I had believed I could do everything myself with my very small team of help, but found that this wasn't totally true. I needed way more help administratively than I had. I also needed to grow my team of technical people and to solidify my so-far scattershot virtual contractors into some kind of cohesive team. And I had to do it quickly and decisively.

This was a huge turning point in my business; it functioned as a crucible to quickly burn off some old ways of thinking and working. It demanded that I grow myself fast and my business alongside.

I bring this up because sometimes we can get so caught up in the pursuit of a goal that we don't know how to live with it when our long-held goal comes true. Many people wish for sudden, rapid, massive success, but find when it comes, they don't know how to deal with it, and it feels overwhelming and way too stressful.

Now, as my business has re-stabilized after hiring some new people and learning how to manage them, I can see that without my team, I could not be serving my clients as well as I am. The work that I am best at is bigger strategy and developing systems to help my clients reach their business goals. This is where I want to focus and where I tend to shine.

I would not be able to focus on doing this kind of work without the support of a growing team of people.

Based on my experiences of the past year, I would suggest that you, too, can make more money if you are open to hiring more help, so you can focus on the most profitable and fulfilling services in your business that only you can do.

In the big picture, your job as a business owner is to streamline the process of earning, such that you can stabilize your business and enjoy the benefits of greater clarity, confidence, and cash.

I'd like to show you next how some of my clients are doing just that.

Chapter 17
CASE STUDIES

IN MY BUSINESS, I've had the distinct pleasure of working with some of the most well-known authors, speakers, and consultants working today. These are people whose communities number in the hundreds of thousands and are definitely people you know by name. At the same time, I've also had the distinct pleasure of working with passionate and committed business owners who may not be super famous (yet), but who are contributing to the world and building strong businesses in a laudable and notable way.

I wanted to utilize this chapter to introduce you to some of my clients and the success they have experienced in terms of their own profitable popularity.

I'll begin by sharing four client case studies and then sharing a fifth case study with you, one from my own business portfolio.

If you wanted to view the videos of these instead of or in addition to reading them here, I invite you to do that through this link: http://profitablepopularity.com/hire-me/client-case-studies

In the event you want to read about them here, let's begin:

CASE STUDY #1
Lisa Murrell
http://www.EquineAlchemy.com

Lisa is a leadership coach and trainer who also offers equine facilitated coaching and equine facilitated coach training.

We worked together for about three months within the framework of this case study.

When we began working together, Lisa stated as her goal that she wanted to increase the number of people signing up for her mailing list, and that she wanted to increase the number of registrations for an upcoming preview call she was offering to promote her equine facilitated coach training program.

We began by setting up tracking and metrics for her stated goal. Then we targeted the best keyword according to search volume and competition. We identified her best content and began to reshape it for syndication. We then syndicated her content across the Internet. We actively worked Lisa's existing marketing channels, including her newsletter and social media.

Lisa was really a dream client because she basically said, "Do whatever you think will work. I'm really open to your ideas and just want to see how this works."

I love when a client says this to me; it leaves a lot of space for creativity.

Here are the results we obtained in this three-month time frame:

- ✓ We placed her email subscription page to the second page of Google. This means that anytime people were searching in Google for terms related to equine coaching or equine alchemy, they would potentially see her listing. This meant that her business was now in front of people who were looking for someone like her, but didn't know of her yet.

- ✓ We activated more of her existing newsletter and social media contacts into her business.
- ✓ Overall, we more than doubled the size of her preview call attendance and number of people on her email list. While Lisa already had good branded traffic, by adding in the search engine piece, we were able to double her visibility.

Even now, her site ranks #3 on Google for the term "equine coaching" which is highly targeted to her business. Before we began working together, her site was not found in the first ten pages of search results.

The thing to understand about this, also, is that this investment in search engine ranking that Lisa made has and will have ongoing benefits to her business. Remember, every little bit helps contribute to a stronger whole.

What this example also shows is you can use content and search marketing to actively find and attract people in even the most unique and tiniest of niches. Usually, the people who are interested in a topic such as equine coaching are very passionate about it. It is a smaller and somewhat unique niche.

The idea is to use content and search marketing technologies to put your business in front of people who are searching for what you offer. These people don't know who you are yet. Clearly, people who didn't know Lisa weren't going to the search engines and typing, "I want to learn how to become an equine coach. Let me randomly search and see if there is a woman named Lisa who offers this kind of program." They weren't doing that. But by placing your business in the search engines, you are putting your business in front of that "river of traffic" I described earlier. This represents a group of people who are already looking for you.

CASE STUDY #2
Lissa Boles
http://www.TheSoulMap.com

Lissa Boles offers a unique set of business services which focus on reading your astrological chart in order to uncover your life, business, and soul purpose. She is extremely skilled and her SoulMap (TM) readings are life-changing. Lissa had identified a unique astrological configuration related to the planet Jupiter, and she was offering a full teleseminar series exploring this: The Jupiter Midas Effect.

Lissa had created significant results when she initially promoted this event, before we began working together. She was offering the event again and wanted my help in expanding her results even further.

Our main goal for our work together in this three-month period was to increase attendee signups for this event, the Jupiter Midas Effect Two, over the already outstanding results that Lissa created for Jupiter Midas One.

We began by setting up metrics and tracking for her stated goal. We targeted the best keywords. Lissa did a noteworthy job of shaping her content for syndication. We repurposed content from Jupiter Midas One, and the content we syndicated included audios, videos, and text. We built authority for the Jupiter Midas website by increasing backlinks to the site, some of which came from this content syndication.

Lissa was amazing to work with on many levels. She provided me such carefully crafted content, and it was really powerful. She spent time going through all of her videos and transcripts from the initial event, focusing on selecting the best content and making it persuasive.

Here are the results we obtained in this three-month time frame:

- ✓ We obtained two search engine listings on page two of Google. This improved ranking brought more visitors to her website and increased event subscriptions.
- ✓ We increased the number of attendees by almost 14% in the two and a half months we worked together.
- ✓ Content and search marketing was the single best individual source of new signups. It outperformed every other marketing channel, including affiliates, social media, and speaker promotions. By itself, it brought more new subscribers than several other methods combined.

Lissa used the proceeds from this event to donate money towards the rebuilding of her home town, which had been destroyed earlier in the year by a tornado.

Content and search marketing lets you do more great work because it puts you out in front of people who want to do great work with you.

CASE STUDY #3
Mark Silver
http://www.HeartofBusiness.com

Mark Silver is a Sufi teacher who offers programs focused on spiritual business teachings. His goal is to help his clients make a profit while staying connected to their Spirit. The goal of our work together has been to increase his search engine rankings and email subscriptions.

These kinds of goals are really excellent for traffic generation work because it's very rare that someone will come directly from the search engines and make a big purchase on their first visit. It can and does happen, but it's more the exception than the rule.

More common is that people join your newsletter or sign up for something free to begin the relationship.

What we did together was, again, set up metrics and tracking. We targeted several relevant keywords. We syndicated content through the Internet, and we increased his website's authority by building backlinks. We tested and improved conversion, watching how many people were visiting the page and how many were signing up.

Mark is a dream client because he has no ego tied up in anything. He is very open to my ideas and willing to do whatever it takes to reach his goals.

He often says, "If you think this is going to work better, let's try it. No matter if I stayed up all night writing that copy, doesn't matter, we can do something else." It's really, really nice in this kind of work because it is exploratory to some degree. I have data that shows that we can get some results with some predictability, but we don't know all the time that even if we can get it in front of people, they will click. Sometimes we have to say that we are getting it in front of people, they're not clicking like we expect, what can we do? Mark has really been wonderful because he is very open; he really wants to go with what the data says.

Here are the results we've obtained so far:

- ✓ We have obtained several first page listings on Google, on terms highly relevant to his business.
- ✓ We have increased his newsletter subscribers.
- ✓ His higher search engine placement means that his business is in front of thousands more people each month, and that creates greater visibility and visitors 24 hours a day, 7 days a week, 365 days a year without extra work. Yes, we have to maintain these listings, but aside from this, his business is regularly in front of many more people than he would be able to regularly sustain on his own.

And this will continue; we have other key words that we are targeting. We will just get another channel and another channel and another channel and so on. Each of these channels represents a flow of new people into his business.

What that shows is that content and search marketing can help you reach your business goals more quickly with less ongoing work.

CASE STUDY #4
Casey Truffo
http://www.BeAWealthyTherapist.com

• •

Casey Truffo is a psychotherapist who coaches other psychotherapists on how to build an insurance-free and thriving private practice. Casey has an impressive number of success stories and is a thought leader in her field.

She wanted to build her online visibility and attract more clients from the Internet.

So we first set up metrics and tracking for her goals. We targeted sets of relevant keywords. We syndicated her content across the Internet.

Casey is amazing to work with because she takes action quickly. She immediately jumps on board when I suggest a new approach, and she keeps careful track of her numbers and is fluent in what they mean.

Here are the results we've obtained so far:

- ✓ Multiple #1 listings in Google. This has increased her visibility, site traffic, opportunities and client inquiries.
- ✓ Increased number of subscribers to her email newsletter. She recently shared with me that her number of subscribers in a one month period was now three times higher this year than it was in the same time period last year, before we began working together.

Perhaps the best way to bring home the significance of these results is to read it in Casey's own words:

"I literally have Rachna on speed-dial. Before Rachna helped us, in an average month, we'd sell one or two products we weren't promoting and I'd get one unsolicited request for coaching. But after Rachna? Well, just yesterday I sold 2 courses in our store, talked to 3 people about coaching, and helped my team with about a dozen other requests for products and services."

What this shows is that, with a system in place, you can convert greater visibility into greater profitability.

CASE STUDY #5
Rachna Jain
http://www.CompleteYourDissertation.com

I mentioned earlier in this book that I've built my businesses mainly by search engine marketing. I wanted to share one of my niche coaching businesses here.

One of my niche businesses is www.CompleteYourDissertation.com. It's a dissertation coaching business that helps graduate students complete their dissertations.

I will tell you right now, if you go to the site, it is ugly. So don't hold that against me. You will go there and you will be like, "Wow, no branding whatsoever." And you wouldn't be wrong.

But what I wanted to show you is there is strategy behind this business, and content and search marketing has supported that fully. It is more than a six-figure business purely from that.

Here is the strategy:
- Highly niched
- Low competition

- Very high value content: specific, relevant, evergreen, and repurposed
- Long term clients—often a year or more
- National and international client base—have worked with clients from Europe, the UK, Malaysia, Singapore, Saudi Arabia, Turkey, and so on.
- Generally recession proof market
- Meaningful service: people will pay for it
- Flexible scheduling: set up coaching on your own hours

Here are the authority building tactics:
- Blogging
- Speaking
- List Building
- Product Creation
- Expert Positioning
- Evolution of Services
- Social Proof

So you visit this website which is sort of ugly, and you'll see on the first page, "You have come to the best place on the Internet for dissertation coaching. You can read my dissertation newsletter. You won't find anyone who can help you as we can. You want to stay; you want to stick around for a while."

There is expert positioning right from the beginning. I've made it a high priority to collect testimonials and social proof. It's not easy in this market because there is often a high degree of shame that they need coaching to finish their dissertations. When you can get testimonials, they are worth their weight in gold.

The product and service funnel for this business looks like this:

1. Free: blog and newsletter
2. Products: dissertation books, membership site. The books are about $15-$20 each, and there are three of them. The membership site is $15 monthly. There are members who have been in the site for more than three years at the time of this writing. Two of the books are available in print; all three are available in eReader formats: Kindle, Nook, and IBooks.

    What has been interesting is that as Amazon has opened up international sales, my books are now selling in Germany, Italy and France.

3. Services: group coaching (~$150 monthly per person, groups of 8) or individual coaching by phone (~$500 monthly). Paid speaking ($1,500-$3,000 per presentation). Paid consultation to review doctoral programs and critique them ($3,500-$8,000 or more per program).

    All of this runs on search engine marketing. The site, while not as actively maintained these days, still retains multiple #1 rankings in Google and receives 30-50 visitors per day. It averages about 3-5 newsletter subscriptions per day, and my newsletter includes regularly delivered content plus evergreen offers to buy my books, join my membership site, or inquire about coaching. It also generates about 4-6 client inquiries weekly. In fact, in the past four months, I have referred out more than 50 potential clients to my associate coaches.

    At this point, this business runs kind of like a machine, in a nice way. All the work comes from getting people into the top part of the funnel (visiting the blog and signing up for the newsletter). As you can see, it is a "dollars for hours" service business, so there are some limitations with that.

Overall, though, you can see that it doesn't take a lot of traffic to be able to build a six-figure plus service business from using the Internet.

Pretty cool, right?

The overall takeaway points from this chapter are these:

The first: content and search marketing leverages everything that you were already doing. It's about adding on to what you are already doing. You are probably already creating fantastic content for your business. This is about getting it out into the world in a larger and sustainable way.

The second: you can have more results with less work. Once you take the time to get your marketing systems set up, they run for you almost automatically. They allow you to attract new opportunities: media inquiries, interviews, speaking engagements, new clients. All of this happens when people can find you online and feel they can trust you to provide what they need.

The third: better online marketing can transform your business. As I often say, "Popularity is good, profitability is better, but profitable popularity is the ultimate goal."

Make a commitment to invest in your online business presence in a steady and continuous way. It takes some time to get results, so you have to be patient, watch your metrics, and respond quickly when opportunities open up for you. You can't be too urgent about this kind of marketing, and it's not something you undertake when you need results very rapidly.

However, investing in this type of marketing can build a sustainable and lasting business, one that you can count on to deliver ongoing results.

NOTES

Chapter 18

YOUR BUSINESS AS A FORCE FOR GOOD

THE BIGGEST REASON I do the work I do is because I see it as a force of good in the world. It might sound funny since I've written so much about profitability in this book, but I think about this in a very specific way.

If you're familiar at all with the work of Abraham Maslow, who was a humanistic psychologist, you've probably heard of Maslow's Hierarchy of Needs.

Dr. Maslow defined how we pursue the experiences we want and placed them on a hierarchy from most immediate concerns to more abstract concerns, all within the framework of achieving greater psychological health.

At the base of the hierarchy, corresponding to the most pressing needs, are physiological needs. These include needs for food, water, shelter. These are needs that must be met to keep our bodies running. Until these are met, we don't have a lot of extra resources to focus on any other needs.

Once these physiological needs are met, our next area of

focus becomes safety needs. At this level, we are concerned about security. We want to know that our home is safe, our family secure, our job or source of employment is steady, and that we are in good health and have good resources.

After we've stabilized these areas, then we start to seek to fulfill our belonging needs. Belonging needs deal with our interpersonal relationships—we seek out love, intimacy, laughter, fulfillment in our social relationships.

Once we have met these needs, we then turn our attention to our esteem needs, which are needs for achievement, self-esteem, self confidence, and respect.

At the highest level of the hierarchy is what Maslow termed "self-actualization" which we can think of as becoming the best version of ourselves. At this level, we fulfill our needs for creativity and self expression, and we look to leave a positive and meaningful imprint on our world.

While Maslow was describing psychological health in his hierarchy, I see that this hierarchy can also overlay onto our cycles of business growth and evolution.

At the first level in the adapted hierarchy (i.e., Maslow's hierarchy applied to business), we can see that we need to first earn enough money to support our physiological needs. We need to be able to keep our homes heated, food on the table, and to be able to take care of our needs for sleep, rest, and self maintenance.

Once we've achieved this level, we might seek to earn more in order to stabilize our income and to begin to create a financial reserve or financial cushion. Once we have met this level of security needs, we then look to meet our belonging needs.

Perhaps we seek out new partners or creative collaborations, or we meet new business friends that we like and admire. We begin to take our place within the sphere of professional associations we want to have.

As we build our communities, we begin to turn our eyes toward bigger goals we might have: ones around becoming more well-known, more self confident, better able to achieve. At this level, we might raise our public profile, welcome more clients, and refine our working style and approach.

CREATE LEGACY
CREATIVE WORK AND BIG IMPACT

BUILD PLATFORM
VISIBILITY AND EXPERTISE

GROW POPULARITY
RELATIONSHIPS AND COMMUNITY

FINANCIAL RESERVE
SAVINGS

FINANCIAL SUSTAINABILITY
ENOUGH MONEY TO LIVE

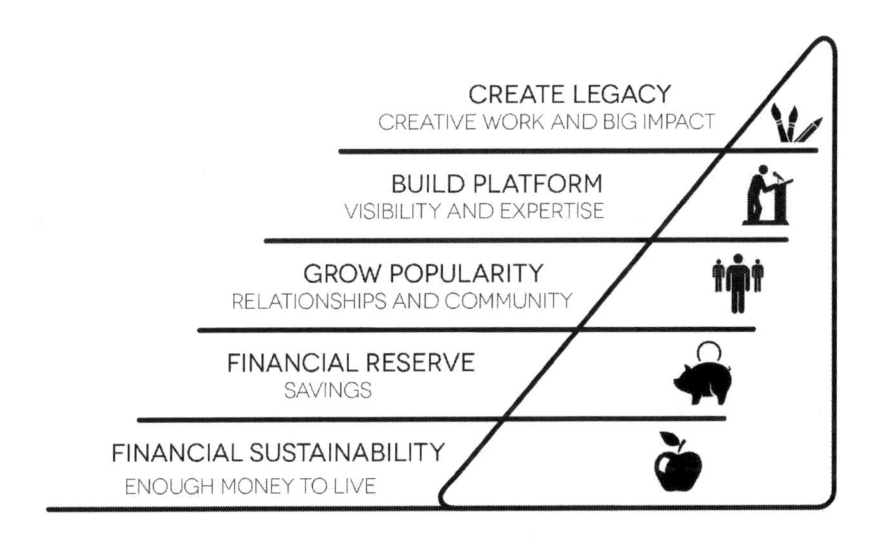

FIGURE 18:1: Jain's Hierarchy of Business Needs

Then, once we've stabilized all these other levels, we might turn our attention to creative works or works of legacy building, and see how we can create a larger positive impact on the world outside of our existing networks and connections.

Where I see this model as being useful is it gives us a way of understanding where we are in creating a healthy business. It is very difficult to create large scale positive impact if you are struggling to keep your electricity on. It is very noble to want to do good in the world, and I would suggest that you can always give more from a full cup than an empty one.

Stated another way, I'm advocating that you keep your focus on doing good for yourself first, and your immediate family and friends, and then from there, seek to have more impact on the world. Grow your business in alignment with these stages of needs, as you understand them.

Sure, it is possible to skip over some steps, but my belief is that you end up retracing your pathway through the steps you missed. Let me give you an example:

If you are currently at level two, where you are working on business security, you might be tempted to go ahead and create some kind of legacy work. That would be moving from stage two to stage 4 or stage 5.

This is possible to do, but I suggest that it would be easier to do if you spent time in stage three, building connections and relationships who might then be able to help you strengthen your legacy.

Remember when I said earlier in this book that I was thinking about writing a book or holding a live event as my first project for this year? Then I realized that I probably don't, yet, have enough reach to create a successful live event. This is another of way of recognizing that, for the needs of my live event, I might need to spend time in stage three—building up connections and alliances—before I can go to stage four, which is working on this goal and then stage five, which is expressing it fully.

Many times, I see people trying to leapfrog into the higher level stages before they've comfortably lived through the initial stages. If you see that your business isn't yet providing consistently for your physiological and safety needs, focus there first. It doesn't mean you won't be able to do the other, bigger, grander goals later. It's just that first, you must stabilize where you are. Focus on gaining clients, experience, and confidence. Focus on creating results with them.

If you find that your business is stabilized, but your professional connections are a bit sparse, spend some time cultivating new relationships and meeting new people. You can gain a lot from investing in these kinds of business relationships.

From there, you are likely to move back and forth between stages four and five. In fact, at different times, you might cycle all the way through from the initial stages to the latter ones.

This hierarchy model is a solid one for helping us see where we are, and for understanding what our business might need next.

You can't successfully sustain your bigger level goals until you've sustained your basic needs.

When we take this model and we overlay it onto technology, I see that technology, used correctly, has the power to help you leverage yourself in meaningful and relevant ways. It enables you to keep track of your finances, for instance, so you know you're building a financial reserve. It can help you make contact with other business owners, such as through social media. It can help you transmit your ideas faster and farther, such as through blogging or other content marketing.

Technology is a tool to help you reach your human goals.

When someone is feeling confused in their business and in how to grow it, I tend to believe that it is due to one of two simple factors. Either they don't know what they want to do (a problem of goals/strategy) or they don't know how to do it (a problem of tools/technology).

I've found it really useful to think about my own business concerns through this framework: do I know what I want to do? Do I know how to do it?

If the answer to both of those questions is yes, but I am still feeling some hesitancy, I realize that it is time to consider not just strategy and tools, but then my personal psychology: what am I afraid of in bringing this project to life?

If you consider the three questions of "Do I know?" "Do I know how?" "What do I fear?" you may find, as I do, that you can usually find the root of your confusion somewhere within the space of these questions.

If you keep in mind the idea of building your business in concentric circles, starting from closest in and moving out from there, this can be a useful visual image to keep you focused on your next right steps.

Bring more of what really matters to your life.

The goal of your business is, ultimately, to bring more of what really matters to your life. It is about finding your deeper "why" and stepping into your wholehearted meaning of what you are here for and how you are meant to contribute and serve.

I believe that everything we do in our businesses has the possibility to make the world a better place. The goal of all we do, I think, is to finally express the truest and best versions of ourselves to the world in all the ways that deeply matter to us.

The reason to find easier, faster, better ways to build your business profitability is simply this:

When you don't have to worry as much about client acquisition, you can focus on client service. When you have your client services running well, maybe you can focus on growing your business by adding more associates. Once that is running well, you can focus on ways to retain your clients longer. And when that is running well, you have an abundance of money, time, and energy that is freed up to turn towards self expression, or, as Maslow would say, self-actualization.

Even though I focus on profitability as one of the major cornerstones of my work with clients, I am not focused on money at the expense of everything else. I want to help my clients' businesses run better so they grow as people, becoming more confident and assured, and so they can make a bigger impact in the world in whatever way is meaningful to them. I want them to have more time to spend with their families. I want them to have more energy for creative hobbies and pursuits. I want them to contribute to charitable causes.

I want them to have the resources they need to fully express all the good they can do in the world.

Money is such a huge concern when you feel like you don't have enough. But once more money is flowing in you create a new set of problems to manage. And once you handle those, there will be a new set, and so on.

It's really about evolving yourself through the process of developing your business. The bigger you become in terms of your internal capacities and sense of personal spaciousness, the more opportunities you'll have in your life and career.

The reason that profitable popularity is so important, at the end of the day, is because it helps you build the life and business you want. You feel yourself to be part of a living network, one that is growing and expanding to enable more and more value to be gained and shared among the community. You are amply provided for in the basic securities of life. And in this space, your soul can flourish.

I believe you deserve to be liked and rich. Those are two pathways to activate the fullest expression of who you are and what you bring to the world.

> The reason that profitable popularity is so important, at the end of the day, is because it helps you build the life and business you want.

Howard Thurman said it so well:

"Don't ask yourself what the world needs. Ask yourself what makes you come alive and then go do that. Because what the world needs is people who have come alive."

And I also wanted to share one more quote, this one from the inimitable Seth Godin, in his book, Tribes:

"We live in a world where we have the leverage to make things happen, the desire to do work we believe in, and a marketplace that is begging us to be remarkable."

Make things happen. Do work you believe in. Be remarkable at all you choose to do.

Chapter 19

PUTTING IT ALL TOGETHER

IF YOU'VE EVER heard me speak or teach, you know I usually end with a slide entitled "Putting it All Together"—this is where I like to summarize in action steps.

So here is the equivalent in book form. :)

STEP ONE:
Begin by reviewing your current website and determining if it is functioning for you as a client attractor and business generator. If it is, look at how you can increase this further. If it's not, decide what steps you must take to have it do so.

STEP TWO:
Review your current community and determine if you have been pursuing popularity or profitability, or both. If you've been pursuing popularity only, craft a plan to start encouraging your fans and followers to take action. If you've been pursuing profitability only, craft a plan to start growing your visibility. You want to make sure you have enough new people coming into

your business on a regular-enough basis to maintain and grow your profitability.

STEP THREE:
Look at your overall marketing and sales strategy. What is working well? What needs improvement? Who can help you implement the tools you want to add?

STEP FOUR:
Do a cash flow check. Review your past three months in your business. How much cash are you generating? Is that number rising, falling, or staying the same?

STEP FIVE:
Examine any areas of blocks or confusion in your business right now. Is there a way that having more data would help you make a decision? Where would more data give your feelings a rest?

STEP SIX:
Do a spot check of yourself. How well are you taking good care of you? How is your sleep? Exercise? Food intake? Water intake? Relaxation? Relationships? When was the last time you did something fun? When is the next time you will do something fun?

STEP SEVEN:
Answer the questions, "How well positioned are you to become a category of one?" "Do you feel like that goal is growing closer or further away?"

STEP EIGHT:
Rate yourself on the seven social currencies. How much attention are you getting in your marketing efforts and in social media? How much engagement? How much do you feel people know, like and trust you? Is your reputation growing in a positive way? Are people sharing about you and talking about you in a supportive way?

STEP NINE:
Determine your business's key performance indicators, and get well versed with your website analytics. Keep track of the numbers and use them to support your business decisions and to back up your gut feelings.

STEP TEN:
Take stock of your business in terms of content production, traffic generation, and monetization. How prolific are you? How well is your content being distributed? Are you attracting new visitors and new fans? Are you monetizing well to the amount of attention you are receiving? Do you have money leaks in your business which need attention? Are you collecting all the money you are owed?

STEP ELEVEN:
Are you creating a platform for leadership in your market? Are you creating original and useful content, positioning yourself as an authority in your field, while also building an authoritative website presence?

STEP TWELVE:
Are you moving steadily through Jain's hierarchy in your business, making sure you've stabilized at each level before reaching for the next? Are you building in helpful business structures and connecting with the people you need to help grow your vision?

My whole purpose in writing this book is because I wanted to spark some conversations about how you might make your business easier and better to run, while increasing your profitability at the same time.

As you reflect and take action on each of these steps, you might feel that your business is operating as many distinct and separate pieces. As you continue to work with each of these elements, you'll begin to see how they work together, and how each lays down a step on your business growth staircase.

I want you to develop strategic thinking about your business, and right-size your efforts for the outcomes you want to reach. I want you to feel confident in what you're doing and how your business is growing, and to be able to see this in numbers and facts, not just feelings.

My goal is that as your confidence and certainty grows, that you will feel more peaceful and creative.

And that you'll be making a difference to your clients as you make the life you want.

In closing, I'd like to leave you with a quote of my own:

> **"Popularity is Good. Profitability is Better.**
> **Profitable Popularity is the Ultimate Goal."**

BOOK RESOURCE CENTER

As a way of saying "Thank You" for investing in (and reading!) this book, I wanted to offer you free access to a Book Resource Center which includes +$200 of additional training, taught by me, on the concepts presented in this book.

This will be of most value to you after you've read the book, which is why I've placed it here.

To access your free training, please use this link:

http://ProfitablePopularity.com/go/BookResourceCenter

It will direct you where you need to go.

Once there, you'll be given instructions of how to access the additional materials.

I hope you'll become even more profitable and popular with these extras!

☺
Rachna

ABOUT RACHNA JAIN

THE INTERPLAY OF human psychology and technology has always intrigued me. I first became interested in online marketing when I saw the potential to reach thousands of people all around the world. It always amazes me that the Internet allows me to connect with and influence people I've never met in person. It's one of the best ways to create income and visibility more easily.

In a business sense, Internet marketing has been very good for me, as it's enabled me to successfully build three distinct six figure plus service businesses in the past fourteen years.

In my career, I've been fortunate enough to work with some of the most well known authors, speakers, consultants, and coaches in the world. While I worked on different kinds of projects for each of these clients, there were commonalities in what I did, and most of it centered around building communities, generating traffic, and assisting with monetization and conversion.

In the simplest terms, I helped grow their fan base (using a combination of content, traffic, and syndication strategies), and I helped them monetize this increased visibility through direct service sales, continuity program sales and individual product sales. I helped them test their sales processes and conversion funnels and optimized these for best results. In essence, I helped them become more profitable and more popular.

My deepest goal in my business is to help my clients streamline their businesses so they are efficiently making more money and creating more impact. Most of the time, this involves simplifying and improving rather than adding more.

I'm the author of five books, and well regarded as a speaker and trainer. I've been quoted in more than 500 major media publications, guested on top radio stations, and also appeared on NBC's *Today Show*.

If you'd like me to come and share my book and strategies to your organization or group, I'd be so happy to explore the possibility.

Please contact me via http://ProfitablePopularity.com and I'd love the chance to connect further.

Warmly,
Rachna